T0077943

A NEW HUMANITY IS RISING

THE AQUARIAN TEAM

BALBOA.PRESS
A DIVISION OF HAY HOUSE

Balboa Press books may be ordered through booksellers or by contacting:

Balboa Press
A Division of Hay House
1663 Liberty Drive
Bloomington, IN 47403
www.balboapress.com
844-682-1282

Print information available on the last page.

ISBN: 978-1-9822-6054-5 (sc)
ISBN: 978-1-9822-6055-2 (e)

Balboa Press rev. date: 03/18/2021

TABLE OF CONTENTS

Introduction vii

Chapter 1   From the External Temple to the Temple Within 1
       – Pascale Frémond

Chapter 2   The Medicine of the Future: Light, Colors and Sound 15
       – Carmen Froment

Chapter 3   Finding a Balance Between the Masculine and
       Feminine Principles for a Harmonious Development 30
       – Dorette Chappuis

Chapter 4   Where Humanity Stands on the Scale of Perfection 66
       – Annie Collet and Olivier Picard

Chapter 5   The Importance of Prenatal Life for the Future of
       Human Civilization 104
       – Carla Machado

Chapter 6   Progressing with the Four Sacred Sciences 121
       – Dorette Chappuis

Chapter 7   The Awakened Human Beings will be the 3rd
       Testament 135
       – Henriette Dufeu

Chapter 8   Prophecies and Beatitudes 155
       – Carmen Froment

About the Authors 165
Acknowledgements 166
Invitation and References 167

INTRODUCTION

Back in 2011 we began writing our first book after meeting a passenger on a flight between Sydney and Vancouver[1] during which the desire to bring business people into today's reality was born. This 'reality' encapsulates not only human laws but also cosmic laws. Human laws change from nation to nation and over time, whereas the cosmic laws remain immutable and unchangeable. They affect all spheres: mineral, vegetable, animal, human and spiritual all the way to the divine world. How is it that society in general, and more particularly the present education system, does not speak about these laws? It was with these thoughts that our 'first born' saw the light of day. At that time we had no idea that this first one would eventually become one of three.

Fortune favors the brave and, thanks to you our readers, we have been encouraged to pursue our writing.

If the subjects we covered in our first book addressed the intellect, our second touched more the heart of our readers and it was thus intended. Many told us they recognized themselves through the different journeys we engaged in. They had the same questions, felt the same hesitations and even had very similar experiences to ours during their own journeys.

And so now is the time for the delivery of the third book. This one is aimed at stimulating your willpower and encouraging the inner transformation already inscribed at the heart of life, of the planet and primarily in the core of each being. To live a Golden Age truly means an age in which humanity lives in harmony with itself, with the planet and the entire cosmos. It is not a utopia but a reality that motivates those

---

[1] See the interview: https://www.youtube.com/watch?v=cKp4diQ7cfo&t=45s

already engaged on the path of inner development for their blossoming and perfection.

Spread over several continents, all the contributing authors of The Aquarian Team's three books are students of the divine school of life in which our mentor, Master Omraam Mikhaël Aïvanhov, encourages us to walk forward on the path of light, toward a union with our higher Self. He, who walked both the path of suffering and of spiritual realization, gave numerous methods, practices and exercises leading ultimately to this union into perfection.

We invite you to discover our hope for a suffering humanity on the edge of an extraordinary awakening. In order to fulfil its destiny humanity will be required to make a quantum leap towards a new and universal spirituality.

"The 21ˢᵗ century shall be mystic or shall not be at all.[2]" Through this work we hope to provide an impetus to this mystical spirit of our century.

Carmen Froment
Co-ordinator of The Aquarian Team

---

[2] André Malraux, interview of December 10, 1975 with André Frossard, journalist for "Le Point", France.

CHAPTER 1

FROM THE EXTERNAL TEMPLE TO THE TEMPLE WITHIN

by

Pascale Frémond

Travelers around the world enjoy visiting sacred sites. Christian cathedrals, basilicas, churches and chapels, Jewish synagogues, Hindu or Buddhist temples and Sikh gurdwaras are all attractive places that fascinate even the confirmed atheist. Yet Jesus said to the Samaritan woman that a day would come when a specific place would no longer be needed to worship God in spirit and in truth. This is what great mystics of all religions have experienced: within themselves they discovered a holy place, a sacred, timeless place, where they communed with the Divine in what we might call their "inner temple."

In his work *The Sacred and The Profane*, Mircea Eliade, a great historian of religion, expressed the sacred in terms of time and location. There are places we make sacred and to which we attribute, through consecration, a role of intermediary between the human and the Divine. Likewise, there are sacred moments in our lives that stand out from the ordinary and profane, such as moments of prayer, meditation and communal rituals. The sacred has its particular places and times.

The importance of the exterior temples in the life of peoples

External temples are still of prominent importance in the twenty-first century. They have been and remain gathering places for "God's people." The Jews have long mourned the two destructions of their temple in Jerusalem, and what France and the rest of the world felt about the fire at Notre-Dame de Paris in April 2019, demonstrates how admired and venerated these holy sites are in spite of the intense secularization of Western societies. Celebrations such as baptisms, marriages and funerals still take place in the cathedrals or basilicas of large towns and are the very heart of people's lives. Some Asian countries like Thailand are dotted with thousands of little Buddha temples coloring the daily landscape. All religions have their pilgrimage sites, attracting believers and tourists alike.

How is it that in these times of Western societies' secularization, the great churches remain a perfect gathering place to convey meaning to an event? What invites the nations' leaders to choose such sites for important events and fascinates the visitors?

The great constructions

Throughout human history, powerful dynasties and dominant belief systems have illustrated themselves by their magnificent monuments. Consider for example the Egyptian pyramids, the great temples in Asia and the medieval cathedrals in Europe. These constructions have survived centuries and conceal esoteric knowledge such as the Golden Ratio, making them not only remarkable places because of their greatness and majesty, but also gateways to the invisible world, the Divine. Indeed, they acted and still do today as antennas establishing a symbolic link and even a physical one with the divine world. The knowledge used by Egyptian builders still defies the imagination and puzzles scientists. The mysteries of the knowledge used by the great masters and companions who conceived and erected the European cathedrals are still far from known by scientists, even if certain orders of Freemasons and Rosicrucians seem to have maintained the legacy period.

Ritualization of the great religions versus spiritual experience

All great religions have undergone a process of transformation which took them from what we may call their essence to a series of institutionalized external rituals, leading them to lose the original simplicity of the inner link with the Divine they had wished to establish. So it was with the spiritual impetus first given by Martin Luther, as demonstrated by Rudolf Otto in his book *The Sacred*. It is known that the great mystics have nearly all been persecuted in their own institutions before they were proclaimed as venerated saints. In the thirteenth century, St. Francis of Assisi broke away from the ritualization of the Roman Catholic Church, his revolution precisely consisting of a return to the essence of Christianity. The call he heard from Christ in the little church of San Damiano before the crucifix was to repair his Church, not so much the external church but the internal church whose rituals had lost the spirit. St. John, bearer of the esoteric message of Jesus Christ, was also ostracized by the other Christians at the beginning of Christianity, and his community was nearly excommunicated.

Toward the internal temple

The great mystics have all related their intimate and profound experience of the Divinity through imagery or illustration.

For Hildegarde von Bingen (1098-1179), Seraphin of Sarov (1759-1833), John of the Cross (1542-1591) and other Christian mystics, it was no longer a matter of external temples, but an inner experience leading to eternity and immensity. This same experience of eternity, immensity and unity is similar to what Sufi mystics such as Ibn Arabi, Rumi and Al-Ghazali described, together with Hindu mystics such as Ramakrishna, and Anandamayi Ma, and more recently the Dalai Lama, a Tibetan Buddhist.

In what Omraam Mikhaël Aïvanhov calls one's "High Abode", human beings experience God's love for them and their own love for God, and from that love, they experience Light. This mystery of Light transpires in the lives of numerous mystics like Meister Eckhart (1260-1328) for whom "the soul must move toward the Light by fusing with the divine Light before becoming the Light," and "every obstacle must be driven away from man, as he is God's temple." According to Mircea Eliade, Light is the "creative power" that defines a transformation within. In Hindu terms, "the Atman-Brahman represents not simply an act of metaphysical knowledge but a profound experience of Light which engages one's very existence."

In *Instructions or discussions about discernment*, Meister Eckhart talked about "going out of self," abandoning everything in the created world in order to "perceive God in the most sublime way." In claiming the primacy of detachment, he wrote: "When the free mind is quite detached, it constrains God to itself, and if it were able to stand formless and free of all transient events it would assume God's own nature. But God can give *that* to none but Himself; therefore, God can do no more for the detached mind than give Himself to it. But the man who stands thus in utter detachment is rapt into eternity in such a way that nothing transient can move him, and in such a way that he is aware of nothing corporeal and is said to be dead to the world, for he has no taste for anything earthly." That is what St. Paul had in mind when he stated: "I live yet not I, Christ liveth in me."

The inner being and the Divine according to Master Omraam Mikhaël Aïvanhov

Following in the footsteps of Master Beinsa Douno—the initiatic name of Peter Deunov—Master Omraam focused his teaching upon the knowledge of the dual nature of human beings. Human nature is commonly known as the physical body, the etheric body (known mostly among Hindus), the astral body (feelings) and the mental body (intellect), whereas divine nature is generally less well known if not completely ignored. Word of its existence was spread in the Western world toward the end of the nineteenth century, through the Hindu teachings of the Theosophists. This divine nature is comprised of the causal body (body of wisdom and higher knowledge), the buddhic body (seat of universal love) and the atmic body (spirit). According to Master Omraam, this triple divine nature is what a human being must know, as stated on the Delphi Temple's frontispiece: "Know yourself and you shall know the universe and the gods." Through specific spiritual exercises, prayer, meditation, contemplation, identification and fusion, disciples are invited to develop their divine elements within and to manifest them through their thoughts, feelings and actions, namely in their human nature, purified through a proper way of life: the practice of non-judgment, selfless feelings, and pure food and drink, like the Middle Way approach of the Buddhists. Mystics have understood this, and their fusion with the Divine, with God, elevates them to such moments of grace and ecstasy that they lack words to describe such experiences. For Hindus, the divine nature, Atman, unites with God, Brahman, and to identify with Atman is the goal of life. Thus they are able to free themselves from the cycle of life and rebirth.

The birth of God in the soul, divinization of human beings

According to Master Omraam, the predestination of human beings is to return to their Heavenly Father. The soul, in order to be truly itself and in conformity with its profound nature, must reunite with God, must be God. This deification or divinization was already the goal of the Eckhartian mysticism. For Christians, the humanization of God by the Word, which came down in the Christic form through Jesus Christ, calls for a divinization of human beings.

In the book *The Cherubinic Wanderer*, Angelus Silesius loudly claims this high ideal of merging with God: "All salvation comes from God. Through love God becomes me, and through grace I He. Thus, all my salvation comes only from Him alone." He states: "The true life of the soul. The soul truly lives when God, His Spirit and His Life fill it entirely, when it has given Him all its space." And "The Temple of God. I am the Temple of God and the tabernacle of my heart is the Holy of Holies, when it is emptiness and transparency."

The celestial Jerusalem and the human body divinized

Master Omraam uses an image to illustrate the inner temple of a human being: the celestial Jerusalem mentioned by St. John in the twenty-first chapter of the *Book of Revelations*. According to him, "This city coming down from Heaven is nothing other than a regenerated human being standing on a foundation made of precious stones, the virtues, and each of the doors is a pearl." The pearl being the symbol of purity, he claims that all the openings of a human being, eyes, ears, mouth and others, must be kept pure "so that the communication with Heaven can always be established." For him, it is a matter of transforming the old Adam into Christ, edifying within us the New Jerusalem through kindness, humility, generosity and goodness. The edification of this inner temple, according to Master Omraam, is the first great work to accomplish so that God can reign in us, and the Kingdom of God, first realized within each and every one of us, can be realized throughout the entire world.

A human being's temple: his body of resurrection, or body of glory

On Easter 1971, Master Omraam spoke about the "body of glory," thanks to which, he stated, a human being can resurrect. This body is formed in the kernel of the etheric body, an atom located at the very bottom of the heart's left ventricle, the etheric body being attached to the solar plexus and to the spleen. The solar plexus holds great importance, as it restores functions, repairs disorders and gives energy to the brain. It is called "jivot" in Russian, which means "life" in Bulgarian.

Through selflessness, sacrifice and divine love, human beings can develop their body of glory, amplifying it "in light and beauty," and thanks to this body of glory they can resurrect and become immortal. According to Master Omraam, it is how the resurrection and transfiguration of Jesus can be understood. Disciples can also form this body of glory by fostering moments of intense spirituality, ecstasy, by listening to music and contemplating great beauty, because they nurture and strengthen their body of glory thanks to their feelings of love and wonderment. He added that "only the body of glory is immortal, because the materials it is made of are of another nature which do not disintegrate." Some people have seen the body of glory of certain initiates who were in states of rapture and ecstasy. The Light then radiated from them, and their faces were transformed. At the end of the lecture, he concluded that the body of glory is a seed that human beings bear within them, a seed that has the "glorious predestination of making them Divinities." Human beings, all sons and daughters of God like Jesus but on a minor scale, can resurrect as Jesus did because God "placed within each being this minuscule seed, this atom of the body of glory." This is why Jesus said: "He that believeth in me, the works that I do he shall do also; and greater works than these shall he do."

Spirituality focused on the Light

Spirituality focused on the Light as expressed by Master Omraam Mikhaël Aïvanhov from 1938 onward was not new. As we will see, it had been and remains central to many traditions. In the twentieth century, Master Beinsa Douno had made it the focus of his teaching before his disciple Mikhaël took it up in his very first lectures in France in the 40s and later, in 1962, when he created the concept and practice of the "spiritual laser."

Light in the different traditions

In 2015, the International Year of Light (coordinated by UNESCO), Religions pour la Paix - Québec, an interfaith association for peace, together with different associations, organized the *Congress on Light in religious and spiritual traditions*[3] in Montreal. On the website of this congress, on the page titled *Light in religious and spiritual traditions of humanity*, many traditions are cited as those referring to the Light. "All religious traditions allude to seeking divine Light and human light. Light is creative, capable of transforming the human being and making the earth a *terra lucida*. Throughout history, this experience of Light has been lived by people of different religious and cultural traditions. In order to live and express this experience, *homo religiosus* needs symbols.[4]"

Many quotes confirm this assertion:

In the Jewish Kabbalah: "Seven lights are there in the Most High and therein dwells the Ancient of Ancients, the Mystery of the Mysteries, the Unknown of the Unknown: Aïn Soph." (Zohar)

In the Christian Johannine tradition: "In the beginning was the Word and the Word was with God and the Word was God." (John 1:1). Well before the manifested light [that of the sun, the moon and stars]—on the fourth day of Creation, God had created Light, the Word, on the first day: "God said 'Let there be Light' and the Light was." (Genesis 1:3).

In the Egyptian tradition: the hymn to Aton, the solar god: "You

---

[3] This congress took place in French.
[4] J.Ries, *Symbolism and experience of light in the great religions* published by C.M. Ternes.

appear beautifully on the horizon of heaven, oh living Disk, beginning of life …you fill every land with your beauty."

In India: Surya the sun is celebrated: "At the moment when Heaven and Earth join, the light is born. Surya penetrates the entire world; he rises each day, each day he crosses the ocean of the air." (Rig Veda, Hymn V, 2) [5]

In the Zoroastrian tradition: it is reported that one day Zoroaster asked the god Ahura Mazda how the first man ate and Ahura Mazda answered: "He ate fire and drank light."

In the Inca religion: Tici Viracocha was the supreme god, giver of orders and creator of the world. The sun god—represented by a solar disk with a human face surrounded by luminous rays—was the second Divinity.

In the Quran: the Light verse (24, 35): "Allah is the Light of the heavens and the earth. The example of His light is like a niche within which is a lamp, the lamp is within glass, the glass as if it were a pearly [white] star lit from [the oil of] a blessed olive tree, neither of the east nor of the west, whose oil would almost glow even if untouched by fire. Light upon light. Allah guides to His light whom He wills. And Allah presents examples for the people, and Allah is knowing of all things."

In Buddhism: the quest for illumination originated from the Zen idea that we are already enlightened and simply need to connect with what is already within us. The term refers to a light that shines, which reminds us of Jesus' transfiguration when he appeared as a great light to two of his disciples. According to Buddhists, this light renders everything clear, allowing for a limpid perception of reality.

In the text of Religions pour la Paix – Québec, it was important to "distinguish spiritual Light, the first creation of God, and the light of the sun, considered in many traditions as the perfect image of divine Light in Nature and as the means to connect with the primordial Light."

The last reference of the text quotes the Gnostics: "Christ is not a Hierophant of majestic stature residing somewhere outside the gross material world, but is first and foremost an impersonal, unlimited being, who reveals himself as Light, Force and a powerful radiating field. The Gnostics see Christ as an atom of eternity present in every one of us that constantly moves us and invites us to seek beyond. It is its presence that ignites in us the nostalgia of a perfect world, free and fraternal, similar to

---

[5] Our translation.

the divine world. This Christ Light of the Gnostics, awaiting to manifest itself in each human being, is represented in the Tree of Life of the Jewish Kabbalah by the sephirah Hokhmah, the second sephirah, where divine Harmony resides. Whereas the sixth sephirah, Tiphareth, represents the splendor of divine Light in the sun's triple manifestation as source of life, warmth and light, in the image of divine Trinity."

Light in the teaching of Master Beinsa Douno (1864-1944)

In her biography of Master Omraam Mikhaël Aïvanhov, Agnès Lejbowicz wrote that one day young Mikhaël asked his Master Beinsa Douno: "What is the most efficient way to link with God and develop spiritual faculties and virtues?" and the Master answered: "Think about the Light, concentrate on it, imagine the whole universe immersed in Light." Master Beinsa Douno gave many lectures on the Light. In the context of my master's degree thesis on the importance of Light and the "spiritual laser" in the teaching of Master Omraam, in July 2019 I identified 134 lectures by Master Beinsa Douno on the theme of Light.

In Bulgarian, there are two words for Light: *svetlina*, used for the physical light, that of the sun, and *videlina*, used for the spiritual Light, the divine Light. To differentiate them, the second one will be written with a capital letter.

According to Master Beinsa Douno, spiritual Light is to the soul what physical light is to the body. Just as nutrition, growth and development of the body are impossible without the physical light coming from the sun, it is also impossible for the soul to expand, develop and bear fruit without the spiritual Light coming from God. Light is not identical to God but shows the way leading to Him. At birth a human being receives the Light, a necessary condition for the development and the growth of the soul. To be a son or a daughter of the Light means to have the conditions bestowed to each by the Light and to use them to ensure spiritual progress through the soul's purification and fertilization. By using every condition, good and bad, the son or daughter of the Light becomes free, finds God, the source of this Light; they are joyous, acquire divine balance within and also bring it to the world.

Master Beinsa Douno made many comments on the prologue of

the Gospel of John (1:1): "In the beginning was the Word and the Word was with God and the Word was God." According to him, the Word is "a divine and intelligent act that manifests through certain vibrations, perceptible by us." It is "the manifestation of God in the spiritual world," and everyone must ask themselves if they are in God and if God is in them. Not only should everyone be in God but God must be in their spirit and in their heart. In order to achieve this, everyone must build a fountain in their inner garden and connect it to the source, so that all can return to Heaven and be One with the living Christ, the living Word who creates, elevates and transforms the world within them.

According to Master Beinsa Douno, Light is an "inner process, a substance that can be experienced at any time. Light is the most real thing in the world, a thousand times more real than this world: it creates human thought, desires; it is a conduit into the spiritual realm and exists as ether. It is an envelope to the human spirit, to the human discernment and without it, one can neither think nor feel." Light is the "act of creation of Nature in all its splendor" because "everything is Light in living Nature." It is health for the human reason, the atmosphere in which it should always bathe in order to be productive. In harmonizing everything, Light sets human beings free, as everything falls into place in divine harmony.

Christ said: "You are the Light" referring to all human beings, and when he said: "I am the Light", he inferred: "My Father and I are one." According to Master Beinsa Douno, the day will come when a fantastic world filled with Light will be unveiled to all, and the Light will come from within, not from without. Modern occultists believe that the one who possesses this Light also possesses magnetism, kindness, and is conciliatory, loving, forgiving. Christ said: "All of you are the Light." And Master Beinsa Douno revealed that when Light penetrates a man's soul, his face is beautiful, his eyes are bright, his hands emanate a pleasant warmth, and he has a pleasant scent.

In the book *Wisdom, Principle of Light and Knowledge*[6], Master Beinsa Douno speaks about the new human, the one "of the Sixth Race," saying that when human beings will connect with the divine world, which he names the "higher world of reason", their consciousness will awaken, and the world "will be illumined from all sides." According to him, the beings

---

[6] Presently available only in French.

of the Sixth Race "will begin nourishing themselves with the pure food of the Word. They will breathe fresh and pure air. They will drink pure and crystalline water. They will welcome divine Light. [...] They will be in close communion with all the perfect Beings, as well as with all the beings who have completed their development on Earth." He names these as "Sons of the Light" who come to Earth to instruct humans and renew humanity; he describes them in a text entitled *Sons of the Light, parables for the new man.*

In the *Testament of the color rays of Light* written in 1912, Master Beinsa Douno reviews some verses of the Bible which, according to him, are linked to the rays of Light corresponding to the seven spirits of God, and he assembles the verses according to the color to which they are linked. The verses thus classified allow the reader to link with the colors red, orange, yellow, green, blue, violet, amethyst and diamond white and their corresponding virtues.

The spiritual laser in the teaching of Master Omraam Mikhaël Aïvanhov

Following in the footsteps of his Master, Master Omraam imparted a very rich teaching on the spiritual Light. In a message published on the Facebook page of Religions pour la Paix – Québec, on March 26, 2020, all meditating people and believers were invited to collectively meditate on this Light, adopting the concept of the "spiritual laser" created by Master Omraam in 1962, and on which he insisted more specifically beginning in the summer of 1980. From then on, he had his disciples practice this spiritual laser regularly until his passing in 1986, and this exercise still goes on in the different groups of the Universal White Brotherhood.[7]

The spiritual laser is a collective meditation on the spiritual Light described by Master Omraam as a Light that is "white, incandescent, spread throughout the universe," that penetrates everything and is "the most beautiful, shining and splendid." It is invisible to our eyes, more subtle than the light of the sun. It is the primordial Light, created by God at the beginning when He said: "Let there be Light." In the laser

---

[7] Created in 1947, the Universal White Brotherhood is a cultural association of people who study and practice the teaching of Omraam Mikhaël Aïvanhov.

phenomenon, particles that normally move randomly vibrate on the same wavelength, through stimulation, and converge to form one luminous ray with extraordinary power. Using this analogy, Master Omraam explained that human beings constitute each a laser if they know how to focus their four inner elements—the heart, intellect, soul and spirit—towards a single point, God, and towards a single objective: the realization of the Kingdom of God on Earth. In ancient Egypt, the initiates symbolized this converging point by the pyramid, where the four faces converge in a single summit.

As the members of his fraternity, the Universal White Brotherhood, were used to meditating together during the silent moments of their meetings, Master Omraam asked them to form with him what he called a "spiritual laser" which reproduces in the spiritual realm what laser particles produce in the physical realm. He asked his disciples to concentrate all together on a same and single image: Light. According to him, this concentration on the Light is the only way to get everybody present to vibrate on the same wavelength, in order for the laser to be effective. He considered that the luminous force thus generated is capable not only of helping disciples to advance more rapidly on the path of evolution, but of helping and enlightening many human beings as well.

To create a spiritual laser, the group must concentrate on this Light that is white and subtler than the light of the sun, and think of nothing else. This luminous energy attracted by the group in communion and with the same mental focus can then be sent across the world through a common prayer for the realization of the Kingdom of God on Earth, a world of peace and brotherhood throughout the planet. As Master Omraam taught that a prayer must follow after every meditation, because uttering such words allows for a faster manifestation of the requests, the disciples are now in the habit of saying a prayer such as this one after the spiritual laser:

Lord God

May all the powers of good be stirred into action, may they set to work to transform the whole world.

May all the forces and powers of good in the form of love, light and purity set to work to overcome evil, so that the

Kingdom of God and his righteousness may be established on Earth as soon as possible and the Golden Age dawn among human beings.

Amen, so be it.

Master Omraam gave the disciples some concentration exercises in order for them to prepare individually for this work with spiritual Light. According to him, by concentrating on the Light, one begins to feel it and can breathe in while imagining that the Light is being drawn to oneself.

The first exercise consists of breathing in the Light, then breathing it out and projecting it throughout oneself, one's organs and cells. When this exercise is practiced for a while and one feels completely peaceful, relaxed and bathed in the Light, one can move on to the next exercise which consists of breathing Light in and then breathing it out, this time imagining one is sending it to the whole world.

Master Omraam recommended waiting until one feels transformed before projecting Light to the rest of the world, because the higher degrees of this work with the Light involve sending it to others. Regularly exercising oneself this way considerably shortens one's evolution, in his view, and brings much joy and pride.

This spirituality of the Light, which appears today to have found a very powerful and unique expression in the form of the spiritual laser, seems to be particularly universal. It exists among a great many religious and spiritual traditions and unites them on a higher level in the realm of spirit. It allows them to communicate in a fertile sharing which begins individually from within and moves to the exterior in order to find, for example, new forms of harmonious living for societies around the world as the Aquarian Age is dawning.

The inner impulsion of the Aquarian Age

To conclude, it should be emphasized that the impulse to refocus within, even if it is well known in Hinduism and has been widely shared among mystics throughout history, feels most appropriate for this new age we are entering, one that many Masters such as Beinsa Douno and

Omraam have named "The Aquarian Age." Ursula King, in her work entitled *The Search for Spirituality: Our Global Quest for a Spiritual Life,* states that we are presently witnessing "a rebirth, springing from a renewal of ancient forms together with a new spirituality that is universal, ecological and mystical." As an observer of the contemporary world, she notes that "As a 'revolution' is taking place in Western societies, the majority of the world's population elsewhere continues to belong to faith-based nations." However, she affirms that: "The need for meaning, the rise in a greater consciousness of humanity's spiritual nature and its unity with the universe exist everywhere in the world."

Biography:

President of Religions pour la Paix – Québec, and of Religions for Peace Canada, Pascale Frémond has been working for many years in interfaith and multicultural fields. With a passion for spirituality and everything related to human beings, she recently completed a Master's in Religious Sciences with an option in spirituality at the Institute of Religious Studies at the University of Montreal. The subject of her thesis was: "The importance of Light and the *spiritual laser* in the Teaching of Master Omraam Mikhaël Aïvanhov (1900-1986)."

As a teacher for new immigrants in Quebec and as a musical director of several choirs, she has been teaching right speech and music. She likes all forms of art, particularly sacred singing and mystical poetry.

CHAPTER 2

THE MEDICINE OF THE FUTURE: LIGHT, COLORS AND SOUND

by
Carmen Froment

Before proceeding to discuss the subject of medicine, let us look at where we are today.

In the last two centuries, conventional medicine has achieved tremendous progress. Just take for example the recognition of the importance of microbes. Indeed, it was Ignaz Semmelweis, a Hungarian physician known as the "savior of mothers" who was the first to require doctors to wash their hands in 1847 before attending women in childbirth. As a consequence, a sharp decline in mortality was observed.

Since then, a great deal of progress has been achieved in medicine and the precision of medical instruments. Today, thanks to modern technology high precision operations can be carried out with the efficiency of robotics.

As far as pharmaceutical companies—all richer than Croesus—are concerned, their advertising managed to influence television viewers and magazine readers to such an extent that they ask their doctor for prescriptions even before they are examined.

A physician friend told me that our parents' generation will live the longest, as they are less medicated than our generation.

One thing for certain is that traditional medicine and pharmacology go hand in hand. They address the body, illnesses and symptoms, but do not yet recognize the psychic structure of a human being the way initiatic science teaches it. In the medical field, the lower subtle bodies such as the etheric, astral and mental bodies are not taken into consideration and even less so the higher ones like the causal, buddhic and atmic bodies.

Nonetheless, we live in a time during which mental disorders affect a greater number of young people, and the solution offered is none other than to medicate them without knowing the long-term side effects. This state of affairs is because, in traditional medicine, very little time is granted to studying the influence of thoughts, feelings and behaviors on the human organism. To justify such disorders, the blame falls on the external world, the family, society and even heredity. If only we thought of the brain as a hard drive on which programs are downloaded and keep playing all life long until we recognize them and change the undesirable ones.

Today, quantum physics recognizes that we are made up more of energy than of matter and that our thoughts and emotions are the conductors that supply the current to our battery, the physical body.

Of course, we cannot stand in the way of progress, as we say, but we could at least open our eyes to new horizons. Humanity is presently at a crossroads where we cannot go backwards, this is obvious, but we have the choice either to entrench ourselves deeper into matter to the point of self-destruction or to wake up to the potential of our inner nature.

An individual and collective awakening is necessary on all levels. Many people are already questioning the rampant consumerism of our times. A social responsibility appeals to young people, as their future is at stake. Simply look at the Swedish climate activist, Greta Thunberg—who at the age of 16—was named the most influential person of 2019 by Time Magazine.

This crossroads is leading us to a great human and planetary turning point. Cutting-edge technology is only the tip of the iceberg, yet humanities have disappeared in the past due to advanced technology without moral value. These changes have long been foreseen by visionaries, Initiates and great Masters because the Aquarius constellation is there announcing the coming of a new era.[8]

Since the main interest of pharmaceutical companies is profit, even at the expense of patients, it is then up to us to discover where our true

---

[8] See the chapter on Aquarius in our first book entitled *What the Future of Humanity Could Be,* Balboa Press, 2012.

interest lies. You would say "to be well and healthy." Indeed, and to achieve this, one needs to consume healthy food and beverages, breathe fresh air and maintain a positive attitude in life. In short, to become responsible for ourselves and for our health before falling ill as it is truly the best option.

As I am writing this chapter (April 2020), we are in the midst of the Covid-19 pandemic. Borders are closing one after the other, confinement is becoming mandatory and there is a race to find a vaccine. A vaccine that may affect our health in the long run and may even contain a nanoparticle capable of tracking our comings and goings anywhere in the world. Are we going to fall victim to global control and lose our individual freedom? In fact, opinions that differ from the governing bodies or the elite group who try to impose their will are censored on YouTube, Google and Facebook. It is becoming an ideology war, a 3rd war, a psychic war. We need to learn to stand up for our health on all levels. Let us fully understand the issues at stake! We are born with free will, the freedom to choose, even unconsciously. We have the right to know and, with knowledge, to make the best choice for ourselves. We must each preserve this right about our opinions, our health, and our spiritual orientations at all cost.

Thanks to a good friend of mine, whose mother greatly appreciated the initiate and clairvoyant Rudolf Steiner, recently communicated the following to me. Over a century ago, Steiner said:

> In the future, the soul will be eliminated through medication. On the pretext of a 'point of view', a vaccine will be invented and then administered as early as possible, even at birth, so that human beings are unable to think about the existence of the soul and spirit.

> The materialistic medical doctors will be given the task to eliminate the soul from humanity.

> Today, people are being vaccinated for all kinds of illnesses. Thus, in the future, children will be vaccinated with a substance that could be produced precisely with the purpose of immunizing people against the 'folly' of spiritual life.

People would be extremely intelligent but could not develop a consciousness, and that is the true objective of some materialistic circles.

With such a vaccine, it will be fairly easy for the etheric body to be separated from the physical body. Once the etheric body has detached, the relationship with the universe will become extremely unstable and people could become automats since the physical body of a human being needs to be honed through a spiritual will.

So that vaccine becomes a kind of ahrimanic[9] force; human beings will no longer be able to get rid of a certain materialistic feeling. They will become materialists in the making and will no longer be able to elevate themselves to the spiritual realms.[10]

Again, Steiner added in his 5th lecture dated October 7, 1917:

In the future, if the human souls do not make the effort to open to the spiritual impulsions, the human body will be inhabited by demoniac forces: the prohibition to think that the soul and the spirit exist.[11]

And to conclude, again from Steiner, *The freedom of thinking and the lies of our epoch*, here is an extract from the October 27, 1917 lecture:

In a relatively short future, children will be vaccinated against the development of an inner spiritual life.[12]

---

[9] https://en.wikipedia.org/wiki/Ahriman

[10] http://pierreduchesne.blogspot.com/2020/05/rudolf-steiner-un-homme-qui-derange.html (our translation).

[11] Rudolf Steiner, *The Fall of the Spirit of Darkness*. Lecture entitled *Changes in humanity's spiritual make-up*.

[12] http://www.eurythmiste.com/index.php/recherche/catalogue-steiner/78/chute-la-des-esprits-des-tenebres-detail (our translation).

It is not a matter of being against vaccination. Furthermore, the following statement only reflects my opinion and not necessarily that of The Aquarian Team in general.

For the past several years, numerous court cases have made the news regarding the pharmaceutical industries who fabricate the triple vaccine MMR (against measles, mumps and rubella) stabilized with aluminum and administered to infants from eight to eighteen months but to no avail. The fact is many parents have complained and testified that the very day after the vaccination, their child became autistic without any preexisting condition. If only these vaccines were administered separately and at a slightly older age so the immune system could better absorb them.

No one reflects on the fact that most of humanity presently lives at the periphery of the wheel and not at the hub, our center, where the cohesive force that is spirit is found. The periphery of the wheel represents diversity, quantity, material possessions and over-consumerism; but it also represents division, separateness, and dislocation. Allopathic medicine does not resolve problems by treating and removing symptoms; instead it should work at identifying the cause of the problems. There is a documentary entitled **Thrive** that was released several years ago that describes the present situation on many fronts on Earth and **Thrive II** was subsequently released with so much to reflect on about the political and medical agenda affecting the planet.

In a way, Covid-19 forcing us to be confined brings to light our dependence on external activities and how we've gotten absorbed into action and matter. In another way, it also offers us the opportunity to bring us back within, to better choose our priorities. It invites us to review our purpose: protecting our life, preserving the unity of our body. We know, at least intellectually, that when all the organs, all the cells of our body vibrate in harmony, we experience joy, happiness, peace and health. But, when an organ is tired through abuse, disharmony or psychological conflicts, the physical body weakens, and illnesses weave their way through. To preserve our health, unity in our being is essential. When we seek this unity, instead of dispersing ourselves, we gain in strength, wisdom, compassion and we even discover how we are all united. We have the same needs: to eat, sleep, work, live and also to love, be respected, seek happiness and express our creativity. We realize indeed that we are all one.

If we have the impression that we are presently facing a global fight on so many fronts, be it economic or political in regards to our health or vaccination, it may be inspiring to raise our awareness above this dilemma with the following wise reminder:

> The destiny of a country is not in the hands of politicians, however powerful they may be. They might for a time delude themselves and delude others that it is so, but not for very long. All those who imagined they held the fate of peoples in their hands and that they could do with them as they wished came to a sticky end; for it is not human beings, however powerful, who direct the destiny of humanity, but higher entities who observe and intervene.
>
> There are intelligences in the universe, forces whose intentions often elude us. Thus even very powerful secret societies that thought they were going to rule the world weren't able to do so, and most of them were brought down. Whereas the ideal of those who put themselves in service to the Lord, who wished to carry out His plans, never disappeared, even if they were often trampled underfoot and massacred. And this ideal has never disappeared, for God's plans are always for humanity's freedom, fulfilment and salvation.[13]

So much more could be said about conventional medicine, but it is on the medicine of the future that we will now focus our attention. In general, education is accessible to most people in the Western world and in a large part of Asia. The standard of living is relatively acceptable for the average population and since basic needs are met (food, lodging and education), the time comes when people begin to look beyond the established framework when they discover that happiness was not in meeting their basic needs nor in the accumulation of wealth. The future becomes more promising when our line of vision broadens and includes the subtle aspects of our being. Observing ourselves makes us realize that we obey the same laws that

---

[13] Omraam Mikhaël Aïvanhov, *Daily Meditations* November 28, 2016.

govern nature and that we can count on them to discover our true nature. Initiates have long verified this in the past: we are governed by cosmic laws that apply to all kingdoms, from the mineral all the way up to the celestial one, including the vegetable, animal and human kingdoms plus the invisible hierarchies above us. That is why universal harmony prevails.

The more we assume responsibility for ourselves and our development, the more we can answer the following questions: Who am I? What are my strengths and weaknesses? What is my purpose? And also to be able to answer on a daily basis: where are my thoughts? (What I am thinking?) What feelings do I foster? Where is my willpower directing me? In light of the hypothesis that our brain is like a hard drive on which the programs of our thoughts, feelings and actions are recorded, it would be appropriate to clean the hard drive before the computer crashes, symbolically speaking, or before an illness manifests.

Fortunately, some alternative and therapeutic treatments remain in practice in some countries more than in others, depending on the power of the medical associations or orders, and the big pharmaceutical companies. One can even notice an increased interest for alternative medicine and a more holistic approach as people awaken and assume responsibility for their own health even before falling ill.

Alternative medicines and therapeutic methods

The most popular among alternative medicine and therapeutic methods are homeopathy, osteopathy, chiropractic, massage therapy, chromotherapy (light and color therapy), phytotherapy (herbal medicine including plants, seaweed and essential oils), lithotherapy (stones and crystals), acupuncture and many more. Each method finds its own place according to the needs and the affinity of each person. Plants (including seaweed) and minerals are rich in special and specific properties. All the elements that compose these properties find their origin in the sun since it is the universal distributor of light, warmth and life. Why not try to obtain these properties directly from the source? The best medicine in the future will be named "Surya therapy": with its light and vitality!

Light and colors

It is said in Genesis that God created Light on the first day, but it is on the fourth day that He created the heavenly bodies that separated night and day such as the sun, the moon and the stars. So, what was the light that was created on the first day?

As mentioned in the previous chapter, there are two words to express light: *svetlina* and *videlina*. We mention this because both Masters Peter Deunov and Omraam Mikhaël Aïvanhov are of Bulgarian origin. Maybe other languages also have different words for the two types of light. Let us go into more details regarding these two words.

Now, when we try to explain something rather complex and finally the other person understands the subtleties of the conversation— a light switch goes on, and the person says "I see what you mean." It is not through the eyes but rather through the consciousness that the understanding takes place. It is an awareness of consciousness.

Therefore, that Light that was created on the first day is invisible and is everywhere in space throughout the universe. We live and we move in it, we exists in it, as St. Paul said. If it is perceptible, it is through the awareness of consciousness and it is only by broadening our consciousness that we will gradually manage to reach the totality or what the mystics call illumination. Where we no longer exist separated from everything and we merge, fuse, with everyone to become One.

This invisible Light is like a universal agent, a gel or glue holding everything together. Shall we suggest naming it "love"?

Previously, it was believed that the smallest particle was the ether and now scientists study a subatomic, infinitely small particle, called the Higgs boson. They even gave it the name "the God particle."

This invisible Light, be it the Higgs boson or not, is intelligent since the universe keeps its harmony based on a defined and stable program; since it is co-creative as life develops from the elements it produces, and finally since it comprises all space to infinity. In short, it is omnipresent, omniscient and omnipotent. So, you may ask, where do we stand in relation to this invisible light? There we stand at the heart of the puzzle: it is through the development of the consciousness that we can understand the functioning of this light. That is why all the heavenly messengers, be they prophets, sages, initiates or masters have been inviting us to discover God within, meaning through our own awareness of consciousness!

To carry on our subject about health, if we accept that the entire universe is built on the two fundamental principles of electricity and magnetism which together produce movement, that is life, we then better understand how they contribute to our health when we work with them consciously.

Let us take the example of someone who is too emissive and electric. That person is normally cold, skinny, even likes to argue, and their nervous system is often affected by it. And if someone is too receptive, magnetic, they are hypersensitive, emotional, often overweight and in general lack discernment. Neither one is ideal because both will end in an imbalance that will bring illness. The balance between the heart and the intellect, between feelings and reasoning, brings about a harmony that is reflected in proper actions, behavior and finally in health.

There are 7 Spirits before the Throne of God

The Bible mentions these 7 spirits. What and who are they?

They are the 7 true colors. Just as we cannot see electricity, nor can we see the true colors except through a prism or when nature offers us its masterpiece, the rainbow. And we see these colors only when the necessary conditions are met. For example, a prism must be equilateral, without flaws and allowing the light to shine through. For the rainbow to be visible there must be a source of light, the sun, suspended droplets of water and the right angle of vision. So, just like electricity that we cannot see but that we use daily, the colors of light are there in the air, but we only perceive them given specific conditions. Each true color is therefore available, omnipresent, and each bears its own characteristics, properties, qualities and virtues such as a Spirit.

> Red is called the Spirit of Life. Red is associated with life and love of all creatures.

> Orange is the Spirit of Sanctity. Orange improves our health and gives us the desire for perfection.

Yellow is the Spirit of Wisdom. It incites us to read, reflect, meditate and seek wisdom.

Green is the Spirit of Eternity and of Evolution. It is associated with growth and development, and also wealth.

Blue is the Spirit of Truth. This color is associated with religion, peace and music.

Indigo is the Spirit of Strength, the Spirit of Royalty and shares about the same properties as blue.

Purple is an extremely subtle, mystical color which leads people to the higher regions. It is the Spirit of Divine Omnipotence and Spiritual Love. It is the Spirit of Sacrifice.[14]

There are several methods of healing physical and emotional disorders with the use of colors. In the world of science, it is known that each color corresponds to a specific electromagnetic radiation of frequency and wavelength. For example, from the infrared to the ultraviolet of the rainbow, the frequency varies between 428 to 750 THz (terahertz). The wavelength of visible light goes from 400 to 780 lambdas (λ). These wavelengths depend on the taste and choice of colors that each person prefers. What we know is that the wavelength is inversely proportional to the frequency and that each element, such as magnesium, hydrogen, calcium and iron, possesses its own frequency as a function of its wavelength.

Moreover, since we are all composed of the basic elements of creation, it is therefore possible to change our vibratory level and our frequencies through colors, even to capture them from the sunbeams, those primordial and fantastic distributors, for without the sun there would be no life. By working with the light, the warmth and the life of the sun, we come closer to the basic elements that make up our body. We can capture them, store them and fortify ourselves thanks to the wagons of provisions they offer. In

---

[14] Omraam Mikhaël Aïvanhov, Vol 10 *The Splendour of Tiphareth: The Yoga of the Sun,* Prosveta S.A. Fréjus, France.

addition, by coming closer to the sun, by appreciating it, contemplating it and even identifying with it, we become like the sun. We radiate its light, emanate its warmth and vibrate in its life.

In his work, Omraam Mikhaël Aïvanhov invites the reader to practice several of the recommended exercises to come closer to the sun, and he named these exercises Surya yoga.

I remember a friend of mine who in the 1980s had broken her forearm. Since she was studying the Teaching of this great Sage and practicing Surya yoga, she visualized the calcium coming down from the sunbeams at sunrise, penetrating her arm to repair the fracture. When she returned to the hospital for her check-up, the doctor was amazed by the volume of calcium the x-ray revealed compared to the norm. This was the first eyewitness account I'd ever heard of illustrating the power of thought in action with the elements provided by the sun.

Nowadays, we find a growing number of people who only eat once a day and even some who draw nourishment directly from the source such as light and air. They are called breatharians and the practice is known as pranic living (from prana, the vital energy). They do not eat any solid food and only drink water or broth, or for some, nothing at all. Of course, to arrive at this level, one needs to be prepared and have the right living conditions.

The power of sound

It is common that, when an army crosses a bridge, soldiers break stride because mechanical resonance may cause the bridge to collapse. Such is the power of sound.

And you may remember having heard about the walls of Jericho that crumbled at the sound of the trumpets. Another proof of the power of sound!

I also remember having read in a mystical book that the pyramids of Egypt were built by sound: the gigantic stones were lifted through the power of sound. It is an interesting theory since nobody has yet discovered how these massive stones were placed with such precision considering the tools at that time.

According to the kabbalists, the entire universe is built from numbers which are themselves light and sound.

Already, one can find on YouTube an enormous selection of relaxing music, healing music, chakra stimulating music, etc. What is rather sad and limited is that this music is often electronic music, inspired by astral influences. When music is composed by an Initiate and inspired from celestial realms, it touches the inner trinity of a being (heart, mind and willpower). Such music was composed by the Bulgarian Master Peter Deunov (also known as Beinsa Douno). His musical compositions, songs and dances are at times joyous, evoking nature, at times mystical, projecting the soul towards its celestial homeland. By singing these songs or even simply listening to them, a harmony is instilled in the cells and one feels better, inspired and motivated to improve oneself.

The more artists reach the superior realms of the soul and the spirit, the more their compositions will enrich the life of others. One will need to first go through the region of Iesod (the Sephirah linked to the moon in the Tree of Life of the Kabbalah), which is the cube of purity so one becomes pure and transparent to let the light of Tiphareth (the sun) shine through. Then, inspiration will no longer be subject to the lower astral plane but will truly produce a beneficial and healing power.

The health of the subtle bodies

After exploring the subject of health on the physical plane with alternative medicine and the influence of the sun, let us go one step further by exploring the subject of mental and emotional health. We previously mentioned that many young people today suffer from mental issues for which the only medical solution is administering pharmacopoeia drugs because traditional medicine does not take into consideration the existence of the subtle bodies.

We also mentioned the influence of sound on matter, so now let us look at what happens when youth listen to heavy metal music. The cacophonic effect of this music transfers to the cells of the body until the nervous system is unable to manage the dissonance. Not only is disharmony induced but eventually violence grows, as does discouragement, until despair finally settles in. How sad it is to see young people living with such sounds which drag them down to an abyss!

I remember one day when I was on a layover in a major Canadian city and went shopping in a boutique for teenagers' clothing. Suddenly, I felt harassed by loud music that resonated with dismal lyrics such as "It is time to kill, kill, kill." It was a real mind-blowing acknowledgement of what subliminal music was! I left the store in a hurry and I could hardly believe the impact that music and those words had on me.

Thus, if young people keep feeding their minds with this type of music, whether it is subliminal or not, one should not be surprised to notice that killings are on the rise, for the subconscious does not distinguish between the real and the virtual. The same applies to movies and television with all the accelerated and destructive scenes that unfold at a speedy rate. The consequence is that it fragments one's concentration to the point that the mind cannot find a peaceful moment for more than a few seconds. Only too often, these movies and TV programs are made to stimulate the emotions of the lower self without any thought to awakening or sustaining something beautiful and noble in people.

It is not utopic to seek what is beautiful, sublime and self-perfecting since we all are on this earth to learn our lessons, to improve. It is our school and the goal is to become perfect as our Heavenly Father is, to become Divinities so we can transform this earth into a garden of paradise. To achieve this, one has to start right at home, with oneself, beginning with the choice of music, food, colors, beverages and images with which we feed ourselves. Let us remember what Plotinus said: that each soul is and becomes what it contemplates.

When the education system takes into consideration what great Initiates and Masters have been teaching forever in their mystical schools— meaning the existence of the subtle bodies, the lower ones: etheric, astral and mental, and the higher bodies: causal, buddhic and atmic—everything will then become clear and meaningful. There will be no more doubt about the benefits of light, colors and sound on the well-being of people because, having assumed responsibility for their health, their development and their evolution, they will each find the ones that suit them best with the purest and most beneficial selection.

By sheer coincidence, here is today's Daily Meditation, June 18, 2020 as I write this section:

Some people have strange ideas about the state in which human beings find themselves in heaven. They believe that they take nothing but their head with them, because their liver, stomach, intestines – and above all their genitals – are not very noble organs. Well, they are mistaken: human beings enter paradise whole and intact, and if you only knew in what splendour, beauty and purity! Just as God created them in the beginning. They have lungs, a brain, ears and eyes, but in another form, or rather of a different quintessence, for forms no longer exist in the world above, only currents, lights, and forces. Everything is organized and functions within them as though they had a stomach, arms and legs. Nothing is missing, it is all there, but transformed into faculties, virtues and qualities. For the organs of our physical body are, in fact, the representation or reflection of heavenly virtues and qualities. If you could see human beings with these lights and colours endlessly streaming from them, you would never tire of contemplating them.[15]

The High Ideal

As a conclusion, it is important to talk about the high Ideal. An ideal is something that either symbolically or psychologically calls upon us, attracts us and even pulls us from difficult situations or choices. Let us take an example that I borrowed from the divine and mystical school that is the Universal White Brotherhood[16] where the methods taught by the Master Omraam Mikhaël Aïvanhov are practiced (which is more a lifestyle than a religion). The example is that of pearl divers who go deep into the ocean to find the rarest pearls but who remain tied by a cable at all times in case a complication occurs so they can be quickly brought back to the surface. In the same way, when we are entrenched in daily obligations

---

[15] You can receive the Thought of the Day—Daily Meditation free by email by subscribing at: https://www.prosveta-usa.com/

[16] White here refers to the purity of the soul. Find out more on their website: http://www.fbu.org/en/. This mystical school exists in many countries around the globe.

and lose contact with heaven, if we are faced with complications or face critical situations, we can be pulled back, helped and supported if we are connected to a high Ideal. This Ideal protects us, reassures us, inspires us and pulls us to higher realms. Yet, we have to define it, anchor it in the midst of our lives and nurture it preciously until it becomes a fundamental function of our being.

Here is a wonderful high Ideal given by Master Peter Deunov:

> To have a heart as pure as crystal,
> A mind as luminous as the sun,
> A soul as vast as the universe,
> And a spirit as powerful as God, and one with God.

CHAPTER 3

Finding a Balance Between the Masculine and Feminine Principles for a Harmonious Development

by
Dorette Chappuis

INTRODUCTION

Let us begin with the following observation: there are two principles in the universe and in human beings. For convenience, they are called masculine principle and feminine principle. They are reflected in all expressions of physical and psychic life.

Entering the masculine and feminine domain is a fascinating adventure. Observing, acting and thinking with these two principles lead to a profound and beautiful transformation. This transformation spirals from level to level to embrace the entire being where the two principles intersect and interact, at times responding harmoniously and sparking creative energy, but at other times generating tensions, misunderstandings which can be solved through the transmutation processes specific to the alchemical tradition.

Interpreting the properties of these two principles is not just about the symbolic language but also about the practical and daily application leading to harmonious development.

We will approach the feminine and the masculine principles from different angles to offer a greater depth and to acquire useful tools able to solve the conflicts brought about by their interactions.

Challenged by the urgency of freedom and well-being, we are often faced by the complex structure of these principles impeding our personal development. This lack of clarity is worrying and destabilizing, and it leads to other conflicts. To master our life, we must be aware of our psychological and spiritual structure because knowing only our biological functions is not sufficient to be fulfilled simply because it is only one aspect of the whole. Having a non-fragmented knowledge of ourselves allows us to act consciously without being limited by some disparaging values linked to these two principles.

Understanding these two principles is a quest. It is about achieving a balanced manifestation within, in our relationship with society, the environment and, on a broader scale, with the universe. It is a matter of thinking with new criteria and new methods. A quote comes to mind from Albert Einstein, who stated that a new way of thinking is essential if humankind is to survive. For Einstein, this was the most pressing question of our times. To achieve this, we must understand the functioning of the feminine and masculine principles because it enables us to be actors in our own lives. To create our lives means, among other things, knowing how to use both these principles under the best possible conditions for the realization of thoughts, desires and projects.

Understanding the importance and the issues of the masculine and feminine principles opens a pathway toward a state of plenitude. Indeed, today, it is imperative to prioritize communication between our inner self and our environment. Our ability to live not only on the horizontal but also on the vertical reveals the profound meaning of life.

The two principles are found in many cultures, traditions, philosophies and religions. Many words are used to refer to them, such as light and warmth, love and wisdom, the sun and the moon, Shiva and Shakti, God and Shekinah, Bride and Groom, gold and silver, spirit and matter, the Uncreated and the Created, yin and yang, anima and animus, eros and logos, sulfur and mercury or *solve* and *coagula* in the alchemy tradition, the symbol of the red and white[17] or again the symbol of the bread and the wine in the Last Supper[18].

We selected two traditions to introduce some aspects of the masculine and feminine principles: the Western Esoteric tradition and the alchemy tradition of the Great Work[19].

As explained by Omraam Mikhaël Aïvanhov, everything that exists in the universe is born from a union, a fusion, between the masculine and feminine principles. So, let us appreciate this meeting of the masculine and feminine.

I. PRELIMINARY NOTIONS OF THE MASCULINE AND FEMININE PRINCIPLES

The masculine and feminine are two existential polarities of life, externally in essence as the relation between men and women, and internally as the dynamic energy between thoughts and feelings. Their interactions define the transformative evolution of a person. At whatever level they meet, the masculine and feminine give birth to life and movement. If one pole is eliminated, life and evolution are suppressed. A philosophy that disregards one of the two principles or considers it negative or less evolved is

---

[17] The choice of these two colors is found in the Bulgarian tradition of offering red and white pompons when spring arrives as a reminder that the masculine and feminine need to work together to create new life.

[18] According to Omraam Mikhaël Aïvanhov, the symbol of bread and wine, associated with red and white, relates to the masculine and feminine principles. Bread is white and wine is red. They represent the two great principles at the origin of creation. Wine, the blood of Christ, symbolises the feminine principle of love, and bread, the flesh of Christ, the masculine principle of wisdom. For true communion, the presence of both principles is required. (Daily Meditation April 5, 2012 from the site www.prosveta.co.uk, "Thought of the day"). In the book entitled *La lumière et les couleurs, puissances créatrices*, the author adds that bread and wine "are the symbols of food that the soul and spirit need[…]. "When we learn to feed our spirit with divine wisdom, the white, and our soul with divine love, the red, we shall enter into eternal life." (our translation, p. 112).

[19] It goes without saying that this choice is arbitrary. For example, we could also have included Jungian psychology or all the works of personal development therapies which largely helped women reconnect to the feminine from the early 1980s or even the Taoist tradition of the yin and yang. Yet, there is much more to discover from the two traditions chosen.

misleading. These two principles work together, they weave all links. They are found everywhere in nature and in the human body. The Eastern and Western mystical traditions take into account these two principles, among other things, to attain inner awakening. They teach that all imbalances, physical, psychic or spiritual, are the result of a lack of collaboration and harmony between these principles.

These two principles work within each human being. Imprinted all over the body, they are also found in nature. They appear under different forms and dimensions. They can be associated with the polarization of the Absolute, of the Non-manifested. Each human being contains within a masculine and feminine part, one that manifests visibly while the other, although hidden, remains definitely present.

After reading several works dealing with the masculine and feminine principles, we can state that these two poles are always presented in a more or less identical way: the masculine element, which is intelligence and reason, is turned toward the external world, and the feminine element, which governs intuition, emotion and instinct, relates to inner life. The masculine force is associated with movement and the feminine with immobility. Together they constitute the inseparable modes of emissivity and receptivity that constantly seek to stimulate each other. They are the poles of the primordial creative force which acts everywhere in the universe through them and brings about all changes. On this subject, the Taoist master Zhuangzi said:

> The high point of the yin is quiet passivity. The high point of the yang is fertile activity. The passivity of the earth offering itself to heaven and the activity of heaven onto the earth, gives birth to all beings.[20]

Omraam Mikhaël Aïvanhov described the notions of passivity and activity as such:

> The masculine principle is defined as active and the feminine principle as passive, but the role of passivity is just

---

[20] Zhuangzi (Tchouang Tseu) *Les pères du taoïsme,* (our translation) He is best known through the book that bears his name, *The Zhuangzi,* also known as *Nanhua zhenjing,* "The Pure Classic of Nanhua."

as important as that of activity. The masculine principle provides the content, but the feminine principle provides the container, the form, and the power of attraction of form is very strong. If the feminine principle is said to be passive, it is because this distinguishes it from the active masculine principle. In reality, however, the feminine principle is not inactive; although it appears to be passive, it is extremely effective. Instead of thrusting itself forward in the manner of the masculine principle, the feminine principle draws things to itself. This is its mode of activity, and anything that is incapable of resisting the attraction is absorbed. The masculine mode of activity is more visible but it is not more powerful. To be active is, as it were, to move from the center towards the periphery; to be passive is to attract peripheral elements towards the center. And even if this attraction is not very visible, it is very real and very effective.[21]

The male-female pair of opposites must be understood first in the metaphysical perspective of a being before establishing the distinction between the two sexes. However, these two metaphysical and sexual aspects are very often associated. Women manifest mainly the qualities contained in the feminine within each being and men manifest mainly the qualities contained in the masculine of each being.

The feminine is the least understood of the two principles and even the most poorly viewed, appreciated and interpreted, and religions are no exception. According to Annick de Souzenelle, many references to women in the Bible

> ...have revealed some aspects of the feminine identity deep within all beings, more spontaneously occurring in women: beauty, the open heart visited by God thus made capable of true love, rigour, strength, audacity, engagement... all virtues to which I would add the demanding aspiration to unity and fecundity. Often

---

[21] Omraam Mikhaël Aïvanhov: *Cosmic Balance: The Secret of Polarity,* pp. 79-80.

brought down to a level of unconscious life, they lead
to holiness when lived ontologically. One doesn't dare
using the word 'holiness' as it has been associated with
insipid mawkishness, and even weakness of spirit fed by
sentimentalism and naivety... belonging to the female
order, of course![22]

One of the feminine aspects that keeps appearing in the different
schools of thought borne from Western esotericism[23] is that of the
condensation and the formation governing the phenomena of evolution
and perfection. According to Omraam Mikhaël Aïvanhov, the masculine
principle has the power to create and the feminine principle the power to
form. For an idea to manifest in the physical plane, it is indispensable that
the feminine participate in its elaboration.

Women are the ones who can make things visible and tangible. Even
unconsciously, they can attract and organize all the necessary elements for
something to appear or for a being to be born. Without the participation
of women, no idea can manifest. That is clear. But let us not forget that
men possess equally within them the feminine principle that they ought
to activate to bring a manifestation in the physical plane. An idea can be
extraordinary but for it to move from the realm of thought and materialize,
it requires the formative force of the feminine principle.

The truth is that none of the thinkers and mystics who
did away with woman and refused to include her in their
philosophical scheme of things ever succeeded in giving
physical form to their ideas; they, themselves, did not have
the capacity to do so and they would have nothing to do
with those who had. It is woman who holds the keys to
matter, not man, and this is why only women are capable
of realizing [...] an idea, a spiritual seed by wrapping this
seed with their subtle emanations and quintessence.[24]

---

[22] Annick de Souzenelle, *Le féminin de l'être*, p. 157 (our translation).
[23] This notion of Western esotericism is from Antoine Faivre. It is explained in his
book entitled *Access to Western Esotericism.*"
[24] Omraam Mikhaël Aïvanhov, *Love and Sexuality*, Complete Works, Vol. 15, p. 90.

The formative power of women goes beyond the act of giving birth. Through their subtle and etheric particles women can nourish a project so it can be realized on the physical plane. The same process is valid for the spiritual realm: for a being to achieve inner awakening, it is essential to use the potential of the feminine faculties.

There is a reason why, in the Taoist tradition, the yin comes before the yang. The yin force is the obscure element; it is the darkness associated with the primordial chaos. It is also the fecundity, the Mother Earth. The yang force is the manifested element; it is the light shining out of darkness. Without the yin, no yang can exist since all things emanate from the feminine principle as long as it has been fertilized. But, at another level of interpretation, we could say that without yang, there is no yin.[25]

It is possible to consider these two original forces of the masculine and the feminine as light and darkness, but it is essential to not associate them with good and evil. Because of this dichotomy, some schools of thought reject one to favor only their preference. But to choose one without the other is to show a misunderstanding of the laws governing the universe.

If, among its many aspects, the feminine means the space that has not yet been penetrated by the light, it is consequently the most unknown and misunderstood aspect of each being and of humanity in its entirety. It is not a coincidence that the history of thought refers to the feminine each time it tries to explore the most obscure zones of human activity. The advent of the feminine pole in human history means the ability to undertake work on oneself in those regions where unconscious forces live. The feminine is then oriented within, introspectively. The condition *sine qua non* is this approach to understanding the dynamic polarity between the masculine and the feminine.

II. APPROACH OF THE HUMAN STRUCTURE ACCORDING TO WESTERN ESOTERICISM

A. Presence of the masculine and feminine principle within each being

---

[25] Unless the feminine principle creates through parthenogenesis; in other words, without the intervention of the masculine principle, as many myths attest.

During the 20th century, the majority of esoteric movements proposed the structure of the human being in a very similar way. It is essential to understand it as it is the playing ground of the feminine and masculine principles that either alternate from one plane to the other or become equally complementary. Here is what we can say about this structure.

Human beings are composed of a higher and lower nature. Therefore, they are a double structure. Each part is divided into several planes or 'bodies'. To simplify, it is said that the soul and the spirit are in the higher nature and the lower nature is comprised of three different activities. These three fundamental activities characterizing a human being are thought, feelings and action. The physical body represents strength, will and power, and belongs to the physical plane. The astral body is the home of feelings and desires. The mental body is the vehicle of thought. Thus, the intellect is the instrument of thought, the heart that of feelings and the physical body that of action. The nature of our personality resembles a trinity formed by those bodies called mental, astral and physical.

According to Alice Bailey, these three faculties are the reflection of three other faculties located in the divine part of each being.[26] Hence, to the inferior division of human activities corresponds a superior division, also tripartite, that composes what is known as the Higher Self or the Self. It is the causal body, the source of divine wisdom, the buddhic body that reflects divine love and, finally, the atmic body, realm of divine will.

Omraam Mikhaël Aïvanhov explains these notions in presenting them as such: the faculties of thought, love and will are at the lower level and at a higher level: to the physical body (will and strength) is linked the atmic body (divine will and strength); to the astral body (feelings) is linked the buddhic body (divine love) and finally to the mental body (thought) is linked the causal body (divine wisdom). According to esoteric science, the meeting of these two natures brings human beings to plenitude as long as they know how to activate the masculine and feminine principles.[27]

---

[26] Alice Bailey, *Initiation, Human and Solar,* p. 16.

[27] Omraam Mikhaël Aïvanhov, *True Alchemy or The Quest for Perfection,* p. 25.

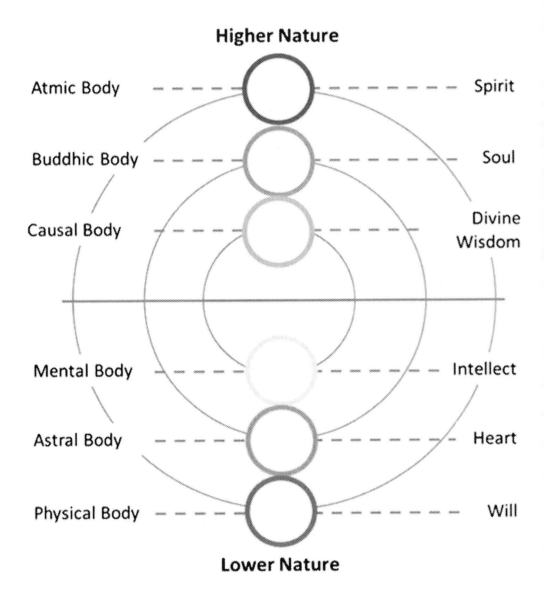

Higher Nature

Atmic Body	Spirit
Buddhic Body	Soul
Causal Body	Divine Wisdom
Mental Body	Intellect
Astral Body	Heart
Physical Body	Will

Lower Nature

It is pertinent to establish a difference between the heart and the soul, as it is between the intellect and the spirit. The heart and the soul are the vehicles of the emotions, feelings and desires, where the heart is the seat of feelings and emotions linked to ordinary joys and pleasures or to torments, sorrows and sensuality, the soul is the seat of spiritual and divine impetus and emotions. The same relationship between the intellect and the spirit applies to the heart and the soul. The intellect is the seat of ordinary thoughts and reasoning coming from the satisfaction of rather personal interests and material needs. On the contrary, the spirit is the seat of disinterested thought and activity.

The heart and the soul are associated with the feminine principle that can manifest either in an lower nature through the heart or astral body, or in the higher nature, the soul or buddhic body. The intellect and the spirit are the expression of the masculine principle that manifests in two regions, that of the lower mental plane and that of the higher causal plane. Thus, the two principles use the four vehicles: heart, intellect, soul, and spirit. These two principles and four vehicles share the same 'house,' the physical body. The intellect-heart couple is a repeat at the lower level to the soul-spirit couple. Children are born from the union of the two couples: the union of the intellect and the heart produces actions in the physical plane whereas the union of the soul and spirit produces acts in the spiritual realm.

What about men and women in all this?

> On the physical plane, man is emissive and woman is receptive; on the astral plane, it is man who is receptive and woman emissive. Man is the one who receives on the astral plane because he is weaker on this plane and woman is stronger. Woman is stronger on the level of sentiment. On the higher level, woman gives and, on the lower level, she receives. Man gives on the lower level and receives on the higher level. This reversal of polarity on the different planes is a great mystery.[28]

---

[28] Omraam Mikhaël Aïvanhov, see *Love and Sexuality,* Complete Works, Vol. 14, chapter "Masculine and Feminine Manifestations", p. 88 and *Christmas and Easter in the Initiatic Tradition,* chapter "Being born on the different planes of being", p.59.

Therefore, according to their nature, men are emissive on the mental and physical planes, and receptive on the astral plane. Women are receptive on the mental and physical planes but emissive on the astral plane. This complementarity defines on one hand the relations between men and women, and on the other, the present supremacy of men. Based on physical strength and intellect, our society could only be one of male dominance. Before women consciously decided to conquer the world of thought and intellect, they occupied second place on that level. Access to higher education gave women the ability to develop the mental body associated with the masculine principle. If women preserve their intuition and become active in the realm of thought, they shall reach another step toward the full acquisition of the two principles. Today, it is men who embark on the quest for their feminine polarity of sensitivity and intuition.

According to the division established by spiritual teachings, intellect and heart are of crucial importance in the functioning of men and women. The intellect has the capacity to analyze, compare and select. Conversely, the heart knows how to connect beings and things; it knows how to gather, establish a synthesis, and its strength is in communicating. We just mentioned that women are emissive, active, on the heart level, the realm of feelings. Consequently, women have the ability to establish connections allowing them to listen to their surroundings as well as their inner sensations. This faculty raises the awareness of women to establish a certain harmony with all the components of life. Nowadays, the search for harmony, for balance physically and psychically, is for them a daily preoccupation. When both men and women become aware of the feminine aspect, the connection between human beings and nature will be strengthened, allowing them to face and respect the interdependence of all living things.

While logic and realism prevail in the external attitude of men or are at the very least ideals, for women it is feeling that holds first place (I do not mean that women are not logical, but rather that in general they give more importance to their feelings and their inner nature than men do). In the soul, it is the opposite: inwardly, men give in to feelings where women reason. Consequently, men get discouraged faster in circumstances where women can still console and hope. If women become victims more easily to social conditions, men succumb as easily to unconscious influences such as alcoholism or other addictions.

Love for women is primarily the will to live and then a feeling. But as long as a woman is content to be a man's object, she doesn't own her independence and freedom. According to his nature, man holds a natural distance from his world of feelings, to the *eros*. His consciousness has its own life and feeds its objective interests that can protect him from the risk of dependency and subjugation to a loved one. A woman, on the contrary, is far more exposed to the danger of falling into a *mystical participation*, or fusional identity with her loved one because within her, her awareness is focused on *eros* that links and fuses. This participation without distance is a danger menacing women in particular after marriage or at the beginning of conjugal life. But when mystical participation becomes a permanent state, it hinders a true loving relationship because, as Jung said: "the relationship [...] is only possible with a certain spiritual distance."[29] Without distance, there are no more exchanges. We notice then that the conflict with women is centered around the pattern of 'taking and giving'. The solution for women is to put their own life at the center, and to seek a realization and a balance for themselves before trying to set the couple's balance first—this balance, in our opinion, is the result of the assimilation of the two principles. This solution seems selfish, but it is the only one that gives women the possibility to be who they are as persons. The symbol of the virgin gives a great example of the notions of freedom and independence as noted by Ajit Mookerjee, for whom virginity must not be understood in a narrow way as imposed by the patriarchal order but in the way to be

> ... *one-in-herself* or [...] *belonging-to-no-man*. More than this, part of the reach she puts herself beyond so adamantly is the reach of society's attempt to describe her to herself. The more repressive the images available to women, the more the virgin condition becomes a defence against these. In extremis, women will reject womanhood

---

[29] Carl Jung, « La femme en Europe » *Problèmes de l'âme moderne*, p. 299, (our translation).

itself, if this idea seems inseparable from the inability to move around freely, both physically and psychically.[30]

Here, a contradictory aspect emerges: for the eros of a woman—which, as was mentioned is the need to unite with another—to be able to access the dimension of love as a relation with another, woman must maintain this virginal aspect allowing her to be herself. Therefore, to rediscover the complementarity between intellect and heart, between intelligence (or spirit) and love (or soul) is a *sine qua non* condition so that she stands in her Divinity and rediscovers her totality.

This is particularly true for love. The goal inferred in a love relationship is the union and identification with the complementary part. The search for this complementarity is only possible when there is a distance allowing love to circulate.

The study of the human structure has demonstrated that the personality is composed of three bodies: mental body, astral body and physical body. A fourth body also exists: the etheric body or etheric double[31]. This latter is so intimately linked to the physical plane that it is often considered part of the physical body. It is the body of vitality and energy. Physical health depends on good circulation of the currents in the etheric double. In the relationship between men and women, it is primarily at this subtle emanation level that exchanges are made. Even if they do not touch each other, when nothing seems to happen between them, an intense circulation of energy takes place. When men and women reach denser regions, those of sexuality, what they do is nothing more than a materialization of what happens in the subtle etheric realm. The circulation mentioned earlier between the higher and lower parts of the physical body of men and women is similar in the etheric body. Yet, everything happens beyond their awareness. A woman should remain vigilant since physically (and

---

[30] Ajit Mookerjee, *Kali, The Feminine Force*, p. 9. At the bottom of the same page, Ajit Mookerjee refers to the feminine again when he mentions the cosmic cycles in the Hindu tradition and, in particular, the *kali yuga* cycle linked to the goddess Kali that humanity experiences presently. The task of Kali is to "annihilate in order to reveal the truth about things and thus to accomplish her mission while giving back our nature the divine feminine spirituality that was lost."

[31] Arthur Powell, *The Etheric Double*.

on the etheric level) the region of her genital organs is receptive, therefore she receives all the influences, pure and impure. This explains why many women have problems in this region, for they often absorb questionable energies. We will come back to this issue when we cover the circulation of energies on the physical plane between men and women.

B. **Focus on the Feminine**

We often hear these days that we are going from a period dominated by masculine values: competition, conquest, domination and growth, into a period dominated by feminine values: communication, friendliness, solidarity, balance, complementarity and transmission of knowledge. It will be true if women know how to integrate the positive aspects of the masculine principle and preserve their feminine attributes. But if they manifest the same shortcomings as men in their quest for the masculine principle, there is a risk that the situation will not evolve correctly.

The situation will be the same if a man develops the other pole to express his feminine attributes; that is, if he establishes a conscious contact with his *anima*. If he doesn't do it consciously, and that part stays at a primitive or undifferentiated state, he will not be able to establish a connection with the feminine part of himself, that is to feel like a man and feel the other as woman (except of course if a woman excites in him a physical attraction).[32]

---

[32] In the process of an individual's emergence as an autonomous and independent person, Jung constantly refers to a being's conscious and unconscious. To these two natures are the notions of *animus, anima, logos* and *eros*. (Carl G. Jung, *Problèmes de l'âme*) (our translation).

In studying the psychology of men and women, Jung discovered the existence of a feminine component in the unconscious of men and of a masculine component in the unconscious of women. He called these manifestations *anima* for the feminine aspect and *animus* for the masculine one. This complementary nature aims to compensate and enrich the world and the directions of the conscience. Thus, the masculine and the feminine coexist in men as in women. The feminine personality is compensated by an unconscious masculine and the masculine personality by an unconscious feminine.

The *anima* gives a man the possibility to establish affective and loving relations, while the *animus* gives a woman the capacity to reflect and make decisions.

Our times have been dominated by masculine values and more particularly by the intellect claiming all rights, underestimating everything that could not be explained, dominated. As Jung states:

> The spirit and the passion of spirit were for the longest time the positive goal to attain in Christian civilization specifically. It is only toward the end of the Middle Ages and during the 19th century that the spirit began degenerating into intellectualization. Very recently, a reaction began against the unbearable predominance of intellectualism, and proponents made the forgivable error of confusing intellect with spirit and attributing to the latter the wrongdoings of the first.[33]

Both men and women possess the characteristics of each gender. The difference that exists between a man and a woman is not a sign of inferiority or superiority but is rather due to the innate prevalence of a principle. In their essence, men and women are equal. The fact of being different can no longer be interpreted as a constitutional inferiority generating dependency and difficult autonomy.

To develop the two opposite poles of one's own psyche, each being needs a relation with the two principles. According to Jung, *logos*, or the masculine principle, has a paternal origin; it represents the world of objective values and interests. *Eros*, the feminine principle, represents subjective values and interests, and has a maternal origin. The *anima* of the son corresponds to the *eros* of the mother and the *animus* of the daughter to the logos of the father.

Principle of relation and union, *eros* is interested by what is personal, subjective, close by. Its field of manifestation is the relationships of affection and love, and its psychological characteristics and capacities are intuition, inspiration, introspection, and analysis. *Eros* brings things closer, linking and unifying them; it establishes human relations. This is the reason why, in its primary aspect of being incapable of living without the other, to even realize oneself without the You, there is a risk of dependency. Since *eros* lives in people and relationships, it always requires living objects. As for *logos*, it is the principle of masculine consciousness, the world of objective values. It expresses itself through interest for objects and ideas, and its field of manifestation is facts. Its characteristics are logic and the ability to generalize and grasp abstractions. *Logos* divides and discriminates. Since, according to its nature, it nourishes itself on objects and ideas, it remains independent from beings and connections with them.

[33] Carl Jung, *L'âme et la vie*, p. 274 (our translation).

The intellect—masculine in aspect—is in fact detrimental to the soul when it claims for itself the right to be the sole beneficiary of the spirit, which it is absolutely not empowered to be, for the spirit is superior to the intellect. According to the illustration of the human structure shown earlier, we saw that the intellect reflects the spirit, as the heart reflects the soul. The error of the intellect is that it pretends to be the spirit, and limits knowledge to an all-objective manifestation. Admittedly, the intellect has achieved incredible accomplishments, but it rejected the spiritual dimension of humans, not knowing how to give meaning to life by cutting them off from other human beings and the universe. Have humans failed in their mission? To survive, it is to the heart—that is to the feminine values of love, fraternity, connection with the environment—that we, human beings, must look to gain authentic, more stable values. This change needs an intelligent balance. Rejecting the capacity of the intellect to only give priority to the heart is not sufficient; one needs the strength of the intellect and the heart, to set them both to work for the blossoming of each individual and humanity as a whole. Once again, it is a balancing act to juggle between the two principles and get them to collaborate. No viable solution, satisfying or harmonious, is possible with only one of these principles.

Many men reject the idea of developing feminine values. They are offended to be reduced to the 'state of a woman.' But despising this polarity is ignoring the many possibilities that life offers. It is easier for a woman to polarize herself then for a man to become, symbolically speaking, a woman. In the fight to gain their freedom, many women learned how to use both—positive and negative—polarities. Life led them to express the qualities of both principles: strength, willpower, resistance, stability, activity, dynamism, and the ambition of the masculine principle that wants to dominate, command and impose itself, along the flexibility, gentleness and charm of the feminine principle, which knows how to submit and sacrifice. Because they are in the process of acquiring both the natures of man and woman, women rediscover their independence. Since social conditions forced them to strengthen their masculine principle, they manifest their intellectual competence (their power of reflection and concentration) and are therefore able to compete with men at this level. And since their nature predisposes them to be emissive on the feeling level, they enjoy greater possibilities than men if the latter do not develop their feminine qualities. Capable of changing their polarity, women give birth to masterpieces of a different nature. One of the feminine specialties— disturbing for the hierarchy—is her creativity, her ability to explore new ways. What is said is directly related to experiences, whatever the level of the experience. If a man adopts such an attitude, he will certainly undergo a certain feminization but that can be contained within. Life also brings men to express their feminine qualities.

Being emissive on the astral level, women are strong and creative in all the realms of love. For many women, love is at the origin of everything, it is even life and the meaning of life. However, for men, the priority lies with objective interests, works of the spirit and science. Surely if a man falls in love, it is a joy but above love, life goes on and he does not lose his objectives. The functioning difference between men and women is explained with humor in the American bestseller by John Gray, *Men are from Mars, Women are from Venus* which mentions many stereotypes. In his book, the author analyzes frequent common behaviors of men and women. And, instead of being a cause for conflict, he demonstrates how they can be a source of mutual benefit. Assuredly, there comes a time when each person must overcome the limit of his or her category and develop the qualities of each principle in order to live in harmony with oneself and others.

To conclude this section, we shall say that women seem to naturally show this quality of intuitive intelligence that gives a more adequate vision of reality, if they can express themselves. Men also possess this quality in their feminine part. This intelligence, resulting from harmony between the heart and the intellect, could open new horizons. But to achieve this, it is imperative to balance the properties of the heart and the intellect, in other words, to balance the forces of both principles, masculine and feminine.

C. **Circulation and polarization of energies between men and women**

For conscious work to be done, the notions of emissivity and receptivity must be considered. One initial approach consists of understanding their polarization on the physical plane.

For energies to circulate, polarization is necessary: one side must be emissive, masculine, and the other receptive, feminine. Two currents of the same nature repel each other. Electricity is a clear demonstration of that! We all know that law since elementary school. Also, the exchanges between a human being and the cosmos are ruled by this law of polarization. Taoism teaches that the universe is emissive, as yang nature, and the earth is receptive, as yin influence. By becoming "woman" (receptive) towards the earth, which is itself a feminine principle, a human being remains sterile. One needs to be industrious, active and masculine towards the earth, meaning that one needs to plough the land and seed it to obtain results. And, according to the alternation of the principles, the earth also becomes emissive. In other words, it gives crops from the seeds sowed. But towards the forces of the universe, one needs to be 'woman': to be able to receive them in order to use these cosmic forces for one's blossoming. To remain 'man' towards these forces, wanting to command and exploit them, is in fact repelling them without being animated by them.

The grandeur and power of human beings is that they can become both man and woman. They have the ability to polarize themselves. Everyone can do it at any time of their life. It is the most magical power plus the most accessible. It is only a matter of being aware. Daily life is full of situations where the feminine and masculine are side by side. Take speaking for example. Speaking is an emissive aspect, masculine, and listening is a receptive aspect, feminine. The one receiving is standing in the feminine polarity and the one speaking in the masculine. Observing our actions shows that we go from one principle to the other but we often are not aware of it.

Knowing how to polarize ourselves depending on the circumstances and timing helps to avoid or welcome things. Knowing how to juggle these two principles is knowing how to create or be influenced, how to protect oneself and avoid, or open oneself and receive.

It is clear that on the physical plane, a man remains a man and a woman remains a woman. In general, this is predetermined. Until recently, it was difficult to change sexes. But on the inner plane, sexes are not fixed. Thanks to these variations and ability to polarize, human beings create. Without this polarization, there would only be monotony. The two principles, masculine and feminine, are constantly active in nature and in the exchanges between human beings with all the necessary adaptations and inflections. We saw that, on the physical plane, men have a masculine predominance and women a feminine one. But psychologically and spiritually speaking, human beings are sometimes man, sometimes woman. On the spiritual plane, men are feminine in their souls and masculine in their spirits whereas women are masculine in their souls and feminine in their spirits.

Now, let us look at it on the physical plane, the body. Down below, at the genital organ level, man is masculine, i.e. emissive, and a woman is feminine, i.e. receptive. On high, at the level of mind and thoughts, a woman becomes emissive during the sexual act and a man receptive. It is at that moment that a woman has the possibility to greatly influence her partner.[34]

In the question of exchanges, there is always an emissive pole and a receptive pole, and this is how energies can circulate.

> When a man and a woman make love, the man gives the woman an energy which she receives into herself and which rises the length of her spinal column as far as her head; by means of her mouth, she then projects this energy into the man's brain, which thus becomes receptive. Man receives above and gives below, whereas woman receives below and gives above. Woman, so tender, weak and delicate, is the one who gives above; if women knew this, they would be able to transform men by means of their thoughts. During their love-making, the woman is far stronger, on the level of thoughts, then the man, who easily loses his head. You can see proof of this in the fact that if you surprise a boy and girl embracing, the poor boy will stutter and stammer, whereas the girl will be perfectly cool and give you all kinds of plausible explanations; she does not lose her head so easily.[35]

On the physical plane, between on high and below, the polarities of a man and a woman are reversed, and this is so with the left and right

---

[34] See Omraam Mikhaël Aïvanhov, *The Sexual Force or the Winged Dragon*.
[35] Omraam Mikhaël Aïvanhov, *Love and Sexuality*, Complete Works, Vol. 14, p. 180.

sides. A man is emissive on the right and receptive on the left; a woman is emissive on the left and receptive on the right. In practice, the place we choose in relation to a person will either allow us to receive or repel the currents of the other because we call upon the attraction or repulsion of the two principles.

The fact that each side can be polarized is found in myth, as reported by Mircea Eliade:

> Adam and Eve were made back to back connected at the shoulders, so God separated them with an axe, cutting them in half. Other interpretations differ: the first man (Adam) was man on the right side and woman on the left side; but God cut him in two halves.[36]

Set face to face, the energies can circulate properly. It is for this reason that in the illustrations from the tantric tradition, men and women are often presented one in front of the other. In this position, they let the energies circulate for their union.

From the sexual point of view, the two principles are separated, either in masculine or feminine. On the other hand, in the upper part of the body (the mouth), the two principles are present in both man and woman, so they work together. So, as indicated by Omraam Mikhaël Aïvanhov, the tongue (masculine principle) and the lips (feminine principle) are united to produce speech (the child).

Previously, we mentioned that on the mental plane, the realm of thought, men were active. This observation is not quite as simple as it appears. On one hand, when a woman speaks and proposes some ideas, she is emissive on the mental plane. On the other hand, based on the quote above regarding the sexual act, it is women who stimulate men on the thought level when the couple is united physically.

In the body, this polarity is found again at the level of the brain: the right hemisphere is connected to intuition. Based on her nature, a woman

---

[36] Mircea Eliade, *Traité d'histoire des religions.* p. 354 (our translation). The passage is found in André Van Lysebeth, *Tantra, le culte de la Féminité,* p. 206. English title: *Tantra, the Cult of the Feminine.*

is directly linked to the right hemisphere whereas a man is connected automatically to the left hemisphere.

The masculine-feminine polarity is played back and forth hundreds of thousands of times within each person. This polarity depends on the adopted attitude and redefines itself from level to level (see the schematic of the human structure). We chose to analyze the functioning between the intellect and the heart, but this polarity is also found between thoughts and imagination, for example.

III. THE MASCULINE AND THE FEMININE IN THE ALCHEMY PROCESS OF THE GREAT WORK

A. **The alchemy or the collaboration of the masculine and the feminine principles to attain a new state of consciousness**

Alchemy proposes a series of methods for the divine seed to grow within each being. Thus, the notion of birth is central to alchemy. This work of awakening the consciousness—or second birth—rests on the interactions between the two principles, which are found at every step of the alchemy process, for example, in the form of the king and the queen, or the sun and the moon. By means of explanations often associated with enigmas, the alchemists commented on the different stages of inner development. Those dedicated to alchemy base their work on the knowledge of the masculine and feminine principles.

The veritable Great Work is the transmutation of human nature to reach full awareness of divine nature manifested in the physical envelope. It is a matter of purifying, harmonizing and animating matter to make it crystalline. Thanks to the penetration of spirit into the physical body, it is then vivified by a superior force.

Many controversies were raised about the etymology of alchemy. In his book entitled *The Dwellings of the Philosophers*, Fulcanelli mentions several of them: of Greek, Arab, Egyptian and Asian origin. Alchemy is a concept and a way of life that doesn't belong to any formal category of the 21st century Western thought. It is neither a religion, nor a philosophy nor a psychology. It refused to be part of any organization or any exclusive doctrine of any institution.

As René Alleau states in the *Encyclopaedia Universalis*, there are thousands of writings on alchemy in the Western world, in China and the Far East that have never been translated or accounted for. The important thing is that reference books have been identified to create common ground for alchemists. These treatises form the nucleus in which literature, history of science and philosophy found their inspiration. Even in the literature of the 20th century, one can find alchemy notions in the literary works of Meyrink, Breton, Yourcenar and Butor to only cite the most important.

Throughout the centuries, the development of alchemy became more discreet. Freemasonry borrowed its symbolism. Personalities such as Cambriel during the 19th century, and Fulcanelli and Jung during the 20[th,] century, contributed to maintaining it. Thanks to the discoveries of researchers during the 1930s, quantum physics emerged; and the discovery of the unifying theory of matter and spirit, a rebirth of alchemy concepts is possible.

B. **The alchemy process**

In alchemy work, spiritual experimentation is the passion of masters and their disciples, and their delight is the inner being as their laboratory. By turning within, alchemists discover the different aspects composing their being. By reaching superior regions, it is easier to fuse with the divine, with the spirit; whereas by going into the depths, the other pole of creation reveals itself as matter, their own matter. The alchemist does not despise it but tries to understand it and give it a new direction.

Alchemy theories and practices have meaning and results only within the universe created by the alchemists. The alchemy nebula with its imaginary illustrations, hiding symbols or allegories, with its hidden language is a world that in essence rarely discloses its secrets. There is no dualism between spirit and matter in alchemy experimentation, no separation between high and low since spirit penetrates the entire universe and infuses its life in all regions of the cosmos, nature and human beings. Moreover, alchemy considers the masculine and feminine principles as equal complementary forces. For alchemists, all levels of the cosmos and of human beings are receptacles of the primordial force. The lower a region is situated, the denser and more compact is its matter; however deep within is a parcel of this primordial energy, a spark of light. Matter is therefore a condensation of spirit.

The legacy left by alchemy is not that of opposition between spirit and matter, spirit and the body, between the brain and the sexual organs. It is not the result of guilt toward sexual energy manifested in the body since it is considered a living force of sacred origin. Alchemists do not believe that sexual force leads to one's fall or that women are responsible for it. They do not entertain a feeling of guilt toward this energy. This would be absurd as human beings would be denying their own nature or rejecting the Divine. Their reference is the Emerald Tablet from Hermes Trismegistus, who describes sexual energy as the "strong force of all forces." Omraam Mikhaël Aïvanhov gives precisions about this energy.

> What is this "most powerful force of all forces" about which Hermes Trismegistus speaks in the *Emerald Tablet*? It is sexual force, since no other force in the universe can compare to it; no other force has the power to create life. Hermes Trismegistus also says of this force that, "the sun is its father", which means that sexual energy is of the same nature as solar energy, that it is impregnated with the life, the light and the holiness of the sun. Its use is not therefore limited to procreation; it can also be consecrated to creations of a spiritual order. But how many human beings are ready to admit that this act by which man fertilises woman can become a solar activity?[37]

So, this force is the driving force for human beings to elevate themselves. The alchemy eros can be defined as the creative love of the world, as an agent of celestial and terrestrial harmony. Eros does not find in it a separating value based on attraction or possession. The purpose is cosmic: marrying Heaven and Earth, transforming matter to make it luminous. In the symbolic language of alchemists, there are numerous images and

---

[37] Omraam Mikhaël Aïvanhov, *The Sexual Force or the Winged Dragon*. This quote is also in the *Daily Meditation* of June 5, 2017 published on www.prosveta.ch, researched in June 2020.

symbols representing the two principles and their multiple interactions. In fact, it is all about that but at different degrees of the alchemy process.

Contrary to known religions, alchemy did not develop a transcending vision of the Creator placed above matter. To alchemists, God is immanent. Alchemists apply the existence of a non-personal Divinity inclusive of nature. This immanentism is one of the accepted values of alchemists; it is interpreted primarily by the representation of matter assimilated to various degrees to spirit. Western and Eastern alchemy hold a vision of unity and immanentism, which does not support the opposition of fallen matter and transcendent divine spirit.

Western alchemy can be divided into three categories. The first deals with the transmutation of metals achieved through the application of the antique theory of the four elements; it corresponds to the Chinese *wai dan* (outer alchemy). The second is about the elaboration of the philosopher's stone, symbol of the transmutation of the being. It is based on the relations with the life of the cosmos, of nature—particularly of the mineral kingdom—and the human organism. It corresponds to the Chinese *nei dan* (inner alchemy). The third category follows the same practice as the second: correspondence between the macrocosm and microcosm, except that the goal is not only to make the philosopher's stone but to reintegrate the Absolute. A parallel can be established with the Taoist masters whose ideal is, once immortality is attained, to fuse with the non-being, the *wu wei* or non-acting.

It is proper to know the distinction between an operational and practical alchemy that transforms raw metal into gold and an inner alchemy whose goal is not so much seeking gold but the sublimation and purification of human nature. The transmutation of metals into gold must be understood as the symbol of a spiritual transmutation, the raw metals symbolizing earthly passions and desires preventing human development. Instead of being achieved in a laboratory, various alchemy processes take place in the human body and in the consciousness of the alchemist. The transmutation of lead into gold corresponds to that of the gross matter within a being into a luminous and subtle one. It is in the body that the elixir of immortality or philosopher's stone is created, as the human body is the matter of the Great Work. This formation can be stimulated by absorbing the quintessence of minerals or vegetables, but it can also be acquired without the adept using any external stimuli, preferring instead different meditation and breathing techniques. According to Kristofer Schipper,

> It is evident that the alchemy of the Great Blacksmith constitutes a parallel to protect the One. Passing from operational alchemy (also known as external alchemy) to inner alchemy is possible seamlessly.[38]

Spiritual alchemy mentions that over the condensation period, spirit formed a substance on which it acts, producing a multitude of phenomena. Spirit and matter are two aspects of the Supreme Force. Matter has its origin in spirit; it came out of it. It did not appear out of nothing, but it is denser and more opaque. This duality of existence—active and receptive poles—is expressed in the opposing spirit/matter, good/bad, man/woman or again sun/moon. These two principles can be found everywhere in the universe, from the most abstract realms all the way to our daily life. Even though they appear opposite, they work together for evolution. The goal is not to discard one, as removing one of the elements of this polarity impedes proper functioning; it is through the meeting of opposites that life manifests. Considered this way, these pairs take on new meaning. It is no longer about uprooting evil and instincts but using them to realize the Great Work of the alchemists.

Alchemy pursues the following goal: spiritualizing matter, which is the result of the interaction between the active principle, masculine, and the receptive principle, feminine. Incarnating the spirit and spiritualizing matter are part of the alchemy language.

The alchemist's laboratory is within, close to what we know as the solar plexus. It is in this crucible that take place all the successive stages of the Great Work. And why is it in this part of the body? To solve this mystery, we need to come back to the etymology of the word 'alchemy'.

> The author of a curious manuscript thinks that the word alchemy derives from *als* which means 'salt' in Greek and

---

[38] Kristofer Schipper, *Le corps taoïste*, p. 231 (our translation). In English: *The Taoist Body*.

from *chymie*, meaning 'fusion'. [...] Originating from Egypt, the term *al khemit* means 'black earth'.[39]

This black earth is the first matter (prima materia) of alchemists. The old manuscripts consider it a feminine nature. Why black? It is precisely this color symbolically used to refer to this primitive earth which, once fertilized, will be the source of all life. Since time immemorial, the earth and at times the moon are cosmic representations of the feminine principle and the sun, the masculine principle. In the pre-Christian period, many earth Goddesses represented this principle of black earth and during the Middle Ages, they were replaced by the Black Virgins. The latter are synonyms of the chaotic force unfertilized yet by the masculine principle. Their black color is neither a coincidence nor due to deterioration of the material. The earth, a feminine principle, virgin and black originally shall receive the rays of the sun and engender life. In Chinese symbology, this truth is also omnipresent: darkness gives birth to light, "lead in the realm of water gives birth to noble gold" according to *The Secret of the Golden Flower*, a Chinese Taoist classic. In psychology, this obscure part is named the unconscious.

Matter is formed from four elements found in two opposite pairs: fire and air, water and earth. The first couple symbolises the active pole, and the second, its receptive complement. Alchemist work is based on the understanding and handling of these pairs.

> The transmutation of lead into gold is achieved with the help of cinnabar—natural mercury sulphite—which is presented in the shape of a red vermillion stone with green reflections. These colors are those of fire and water, the two complementary opposites. [40]

The following example also demonstrates the interaction process of the four elements. It is taken from Hermes Trismegistus' *Emerald Tablet*, considered the basic work of alchemy.

---

[39] Fulcanelli, *Les Demeures philosophales,* Vol. 1, pp. 95-96 (our translation)
[40] Henry Normand, *Les Maîtres du Tao*, p. 145 (our translation), quote taken from *Secret de la Fleur d'Or.* In English: *The Secret of the Golden Flower.*

> The Sun is its father, the Moon is its mother, the Wind
> hath carried it in its belly and the Earth is its nurse.[41]

In addition to the active-passive and emissive-receptive opposing pairs, we notice the dualism of heaven-earth, high-below. The feminine pole is situated below, it is the bowels of the earth; and it is there in darkness that life is born. The earth, symbol of inert and black matter, represents the origin of everything visible. If earth is submissive to heaven, it is to allow it to exercise its creative force; and if heaven works with earth, it is because without it, it cannot bring anything into manifestation.

Water, earth and the physical body are different aspects of the cosmic feminine principle. Being a condensation of the light, they are closer to matter. But they contain sacred elements and luminous essence despite the distance that separates them from spirit. The lower the matter is located, meaning the more it is condensed, the denser and more compact it is.

The first matter also signifies the chaos of the origins. The myths about chaos and primordial water are associated with the feminine principle. Alchemists seek the necessary elements in this 'prima materia' to realize the Great Work. They perform all the operations on it to attain their goal. It is imperative for them to know this first matter, black and feminine, as it is indispensable for their work. It provides the materials, and then they model it. Receiving the 'fertilizing' seeds of the spirit, it gives birth to all kinds of 'children'.

> To succeed in making the philosopher's stone, it was first
> necessary to gather a first matter that alchemists talked
> little about without ever giving the name away. This first
> matter, the subject of their work, began with a black
> substance. [...] Furthermore, they wrote that this black
> matter, they ought to get it themselves underground, in

---

[41] The *Emerald Tablet* was apparently carved on an emerald, hence its name, by Hermes and found in his tomb. Who is this legendary author? According to Edouard Schuré in *The Great Initiates*, the name of Hermes is a generic name, it signifies all three: a man, a cast and a god (the god is the planet Mercury). It is on the account of this patronym of Hermes that alchemy is referred to as hermetic.

the mine, in the mineral deposits, which was esoterically interpreted as Isis sex.[42]

If, for alchemists, the minerals have a great importance to reach their objective, it is due to a correspondence. We often divide life on Earth into several kingdoms: mineral, vegetable, animal and human. In the analysis of the human structure, we observed that the human structure was composed of several bodies: physical, etheric, astral and mental. When superposing the two schematics, we obtain the following result: to the mineral kingdom corresponds the physical body, to the vegetable kingdom corresponds the etheric body, to the animal kingdom the astral body, and finally to the human kingdom, the mental body. For alchemists, the location of the substance that forms the matter for the Great Work is the physical plane (hence the importance of the mineral kingdom) and the place where the embryo of the immortal body is born in the etheric body (hence the importance of the vegetable kingdom).

> Common alchemy practice uses minerals as the matter to absorb and among them the first being cinnabar (gold), this essence of the earth which is the yang energy the most powerful in nature and, as such, associated to the sun. Cinnabar, found in the depth of the earth's crust, constitutes so to speak a concentrated essence of the solar energy, the one that makes everything alive and can heal all decrepitude.[43]

According to Mircea Eliade, gold and jade form the great principle yang—the sun. They preserve the body from corruption and disintegration.[44] In many traditions, gold is the symbol of the solar principle: eternal and immutable, impregnated with salutary forces. For alchemists, the metals are dormant energies they want to awaken and use for their work, which also consists of accelerating the process of their growth. By absorbing the stone powders or the metals rich in vital virtues, they penetrate into the

---

[42] Jacques Huynen, *L'énigme des vierges noires*, pp. 140-141 (our translation).
[43] Kristofer Schipper, *Le corps taoïste*, p. 228 (our translation). *The Taoist Body.*
[44] In Mircea Eliade, *The Forge and the Crucible.*

cosmic zone to which these objects are linked; then the non-corresponding or dissimilar forces are rejected. For alchemists, the descriptive embryology of the metal is the model to succeeding the Great Work because, according to the law of correspondence of macrocosm/microcosm, the same elements of the mineral kingdom are found in the body and the soul of each human being.

Gold and the other minerals are similar to seeds in the belly of the earth. Gold has always been of particular attention. The sun would have exhalations from which underground condensations give birth to metals, the purest of them being gold. It is why gold holds a primordial importance in alchemy work. Gold is associated with the sun, it is a condensation of the light of the sun. Gold is light. To work with gold is symbolic: it is in fact working with the light. The gold of the alchemists rests on the transformation of gross particles of human nature becoming pure light. Gold, the sun and light always represent the same truth but in different planes, and are linked to the masculine principle whereas silver and the moon are linked to the feminine principle. For alchemists, these notions lead us to the final goal of the harmonious collaboration between the masculine and feminine principles within human beings: the formation of a new consciousness (Jung), formation of the divine seed (Annick de Souzenelle), formation of the Great Work (alchemy) or again the formation of the body of immortality (Taoism), also named the body of glory (Christian tradition and Western modern esotericism).

Conclusion

The inner awakening described by many mystical and esoteric schools of thought uses the knowledge of the masculine and feminine principles. These principles are at the basis of the perfection of human beings. At times, their union is the ultimate goal, and at other times, their union engenders a third element.

The concept of the human being considered as a laboratory in which the personality will be formed and grow its divine part is the element that stands in what we've covered so far. This transformation is achieved by different means, like prayer and work on oneself. This double discipline is expressed in the etymology of the word 'laboratory', *lab – oratorium*: a place where one prays and works. The words *Ora* and *Labora* are found in many alchemy inscriptions or drawings. This work rests on the alternation of the masculine and the feminine, whether one is a man or a woman.

All manifestation is the result of the activity between active and passive, the Created and the Uncreated, the yin and the yang, Shiva and Shakti. These two archetypes supporting men and women make them different from one another, but it is in their union that beauty is born. The psychological disorders, the present dispositions are the result of the forgotten ontological model. Without bearing a judgement, what about the LGBT or LGBTQIA[45]? Their different manifestations are variants of the masculine and feminine expression. The people who are part of one of these categories may have been caught by the subtleties of the two principles. Sometimes, we may be taken by an indistinct, uncertain and confusing feeling about what is masculine or feminine. A possible solution to solve this tension could only be the integration of the inner requirements of the opposing sex in a greater awareness of consciousness.

Life conditions bring people to find new models of behavior. The old inadequate clichés are no longer acceptable if they limit people. They do not meet their expectations as they are always oriented toward the exterior.

Women and men who are aware of another order of things, in harmony with cosmic laws, must stand in their verticality. The trials and difficulties of life are forcing us to return within, unless they become revolt and repression. According to Omraam Mikhaël Aïvanhov, it is important to seek "first harmony with Cosmic Intelligence."[46]

Knowing how to do this work on oneself can bring an incredible force to properly alchemize all the obstacles of daily life. This return to unity is possible by the union of the masculine and feminine principles. When using comparative studies, we can conclude that this work belongs to the level of the archetypes found across so many traditions. Being conscious of it accelerates the process of attainment and unity with the divine.

This transformation can be achieved in two stages: the first is about the return of the feminine and the second is the collaboration between the two principles. An authentic collaboration is only possible if each principle is respected and considered in all its aspects, positive and negative. Thus, the

---

[45] Lesbian, gay, bisexual, transgender, queer, intersex, asexual.
[46] Omraam Mikhaël Aïvanhov, *True Alchemy or the Quest for Perfection*, p. 107.

emergence of the feminine pole—and all the associated qualities—when lived consciously is an opening to a higher level of human civilization. And this feminine is not restricted to only half of the population but includes each and every one of us, whatever the sex of our body.

The question of the physical body is important in this stage of humanity's development because it is particularly in the physical body that it is the easiest to observe the interactions between the two principles and to master their manifestations. According to Kristofer Schipper, there are three ways to consider the body.[47] The first is theological and linked to the notion of Divinity. The second is empirical; this approach is related to medical technologies and alchemy. Finally, the last sees the body in a symbolic perspective. It is about an inner vision. It is the body presented by Western modern esotericism and it is also the 'landscape body' in the Taoist tradition.

So far we have analyzed different aspects of the feminine and masculine principles in two traditions. If we manage to go beyond the differences presented in these two traditions and look closer at the resemblances, we will be surprised to notice that the body is considered the field of experimentation—that of the feminine and masculine principles. The techniques proposed in these traditions must protect from difficult experiences on the path of awakening. They give references and knowledge to build and live a physical and spiritual wholeness. This wholeness is described as such by Ysé Tardon-Masquelier, who bases himself on Jung:

> Figures of the other within, the anima and animus, when going from an indifferent stage of archaism to a true value of their potential, point to the non-self within a psychic wholeness in the making. They show what is missing in order for the self to live as a conscious part of an embracing totality which is the Self. Hence the meaning of Jung's affirmation which appears obscure at first: 'The symbol of the opposite sex is truly part of the Self'. He recommends developing a method of spiritual asceticism where the sublimation of the other sex leads to the discovery of Self:

---

[47] Kristofer Schipper, *Le corps taoïste p. 231, (our translation) In English: The Taoist Body.*

'Bringing the dialogue of the anima to the height of a true technique'. [48]

These words of Jung were addressed to a man. For a woman, it is a matter of bringing the dialogue with the animus to the height of a true technique.

The traditions we covered establish a close link between knowledge and sexuality. This link is also expressed in the tantric or yoga traditions as Elisabeth Haich says:

> Sexuality and supreme knowledge are two expressions of the divine and creative force, Logos. The sexual force, an inferior aspect of Logos, can lead man to his supreme form, divine consciousness. [49]

If it can be transformed into a superior energy, sexual force gives access to other states of consciousness. This transmutation implies the participation of the masculine and feminine as we emphasized it in the interpretation of alchemy.

Throughout this chapter, we mentioned the existence of another body that is more subtle than the physical and closely connected to it, the etheric body. In the physical body as in the etheric one, there is a circulation of positive and negative energy. When the masculine and feminine work together, they give birth to a third element: a child, an idea, a new awareness of consciousness. Without the meeting of the two principles, there is no child, no idea and even less of an awakening of consciousness.

It is interesting to note that some Eastern and Western teachings state that the etheric body contains the divine seed, which is the seed of the body of resurrection, the body of immortality. And all the techniques offered by these teachings share a common and unique goal: nourishing this seed by a more subtle form of nourishment such as meditation, breathing and sublimation of the sexual energy by using the masculine and feminine principles properly. These teachings are based on the two principles, masculine and feminine, on their complementarity and their interaction.

---

[48] Ysé Tardon-Masquelier, *Jung et la question du sacré*, p. 65 (our translation).

[49] Elisabeth Haich, *Sexual Energy and Yoga* p. 14.

And, they recommend to get them acting together in order to incarnate spirit into matter and for the spiritualization of matter.

> The fruit of their union (of the two principles) is the body of light [...]. It is the plenitude of the circle: all virtues are united in perfect harmony, whereas they were opposed before. This pleroma symbolises the conciliation of the opposites, harmony between opposites.[50]

According to Omraam Mikhaël Aïvanhov, the body of light or body of glory is nourished by thoughts, feelings and superior states of consciousness (see schematic presented in the sacred part of Western esotericism). To develop this subtle body, it is necessary to work with the two principles, particularly in the etheric because

> The etheric body [...] penetrates the physical body but, at the same time, has ramifications in the higher regions, and it communicates the forces it receives from these higher regions to the physical body. So, like plants, it vivifies matter by bringing out its hidden qualities. It serves as an intermediary between the physical body and the subtle bodies.[51]

This body has a remarkably close connection with the different elements of nature (water, trees, etc.). It is also nourished or impoverished in the context of exchanges between men and women, hence the importance of knowing the circulation of the sexual energies in the etheric body so as to strengthen it and nourish the seed of light buried in the solar plexus of each being. So, the knowledge of the masculine and feminine principles is not only limited to the physical plane, but it comprises all the bodies of the human being. It is truly a quest!

---

[50] Cahiers de l'Hermétisme, *L'androgyne*, p. 160 (our translation).
[51] Omraam Mikhaël Aïvanhov, *Christmas and Easter in the Initiatic Tradition*, see chapter: "The Body of Glory", pp. 127-154. The quote is on page 129.

I become aware of my masculinity
I become aware of my femininity

I respect my femininity
I respect my masculinity

I cooperate with these two principles
in order to blossom, to live in joy and harmony
and to become light.

Biography:

Life is a crystal with a thousand facets. Dorette Chappuis seeks to discover some of those facets: languages (German, English, Russian, Chinese and Spanish), exchanges with people (translation, interpretation, teaching youth and travel), attitudes, cultures, and religions (doctorate in comparative religious studies from Lausanne University in Switzerland), physical and psychic well-being (yoga teacher at Yoga Switzerland), spiritual inner quest (interested in spiritual teachings in particular the one of Omraam Mikhaël Aïvanhov).

Bibliography:

Bailey, A., 1922. *Initiation, Human and Solar,* Lucis Publishing Company, New Jersey.

Bonardel, F. 2011. *La voie hermétique*, Paris, Éditions Dervy.

Cahiers de l'Hermétisme, 1986. *L'androgyne dans la littérature*, Paris, Albin Michel.

Chia, Mantak, 2016. *L'alchimie de l'énergie sexuelle*, Paris, Guy Trédaniel.

Eliade, M., 1974. *Traité d'histoire des religions,* Paris, Payot.

Eliade, M., 1979, *The Forge and the Crucible*, 1979, University of Chicago Press.

Faivre, A., 1994. *Access to Western Esotericism,* Suny Series, Western Esoteric Traditions, State University of New York.

Faivre, A., 2007. Voir *L'ésotérisme*, Paris, PUF, coll. « Que sais-je ? » 4e édition, revue et corrigée.

Fulcanelli, 1999. *The Dwellings of the Philosophers*, Archive Pr & Communications.

Gray, J., 1992. *Men are from Mars, Women are from Venus*, Harper Collins.

Haich, E., 1991. *Sexual Energy and Yoga*, 1991, Santa Fe (NM), Aurora Press.

Huynen, J., 1972. *L'énigme des vierges noires*, Paris, Ed. Robert Laffont, Louis Musin Ed.

Javary, C, 2018. *Yin Yang La dynamique du monde*, Paris, Albin Michel.

Jung, C.G., 1960. *Problèmes de l'âme,* Paris, Buchet-Chastel.

Jung, C.G., 1971. *Les Racines de la conscience,* Paris, Buchet-Chastel.

Jung, C.G., 1996. « La femme en Europe », in *Problèmes de l'âme moderne,* Paris, Éditions Buchet-Chastel.

Lysebeth Van, A., 2011. *Tantra, The Cult of the Feminine*, Delhi, Motilal Banarsidass.

Mookerjee, A., 1988. *Kali, The Feminine Force,* Rochester Vermont, Destiny Books.

Normand, H., 1985. *Les Maîtres du Tao,* Paris, Éd. du Félin.

Omraam Mikhaël Aïvanhov, 2008 & 2009. *Love and Sexuality*, Volumes 14 & 15, Prosveta S.A., Fréjus.

Omraam Mikhaël Aïvanhov, 1984. *Christmas and Easter in the Initiatic Tradition,* Prosveta S.A., Fréjus.

Omraam Mikhaël Aïvanhov, 1988. *True Alchemy or the Quest for Perfection,* Prosveta S.A., Fréjus.

Omraam Mikhaël Aïvanhov, 1996. *Cosmic Balance: The Secret of Polarity*, Prosveta S.A., Fréjus.

Omraam Mikhaël Aïvanhov, 2018. *La lumière et les couleurs, puissances créatrices*, Prosveta S.A., Fréjus.

Powell, A., 1969. *The Etheric Double,* London, The Theosophical Publishing House LTD.

Schipper, K., 1982. *The Taoist Body*, 1994, University of California Press.

Schuré, E., 1989. *The Great Initiates: A Study of the Secret History of Religions*, Steiner Books.

Souzenelle de, A., 1997. *Le féminin de l'être*, Paris, Spiritualités Vivantes, Albin Michel.

Steiner, R., 1988. *Anthroposophie, une cosmosophie,* Lausanne, Ed. Anthroposophiques romandes.

Tardon-Masquelier, Y., 1998. *Jung et la question du sacré*, Paris, Spiritualités vivantes, Albin Michel.

Tchouang-tseu, 1950. *Les pères du taoïsme*, Cathasia, trad. by Wieger, Tchouang-tseu XXI.

Zhuangzi, 2013. *The Complete Works of Zhuangzi*, trad. by Burton Watson, Columbia University Press, Columbia

CHAPTER 4

WHERE HUMANITY STANDS ON THE SCALE OF PERFECTION

by
Annie Collet and Olivier Picard

Introduction

Today's humanity is in the 5th RACE (or great Humanity), as defined below. We are more precisely at the end of the 5th Culture (or Civilization) of this 5th RACE: that of Western Europe, as you can see on the synoptic table presented in this chapter.

We are also at the spiritual dawn of the 6th Culture of this 5th RACE. The horizon is already showing its colors by the premises and the stirrings that can be felt coming from all angles. They will drive away the hard-core materialism that has brought the decadence we are presently witnessing, and will bring an innovative and regenerating current from the spiritual plane, which, as always, guides and directs everything.

This table summarizes the entire path of human perfection in accordance with that of their planet, the Earth, over a 'Period' of the Earth, which itself is contained in a much larger cycle.

As for the schematic, it synthetizes the Periods (or Incarnations) of the Earth and allows for a broader vision of this infinite path, which can only be traced by divine hands.

LIFE UNFOLDS IN A SPIRAL

The synoptic table is only intended as an overview.

Presented in a linear way for ease of reading, it does not, however, reflect reality since life evolves in a spiral. Yet everyone will understand that we could not present all the notions of this table if we had written it in a spiral format!

FOUR GREAT SPIRITUAL MOVEMENTS IN THE INITIATIC TRADITION

It is also a modest attempt to synthesize what is known as the 'Tradition or initiatic science', still propagated nowadays through the four most reliable great spiritual movements:

- Theosophy
- Anthroposophy
- Rose Cross
- Universal White Brotherhood

Everything mentioned in this chapter therefore refers to the Tradition or initiatic science.

DETAILS OF THE TABLE (see the folded color table after page 72)

This table is likely not yet perfect in every detail, for it is not easy to review the truths of these four esoteric schools, to decode and associate everything in a chronological order without omitting many things.

The dates and details that often vary reflect the mentalities of those attempting to capture some truths even with their greatest sincerity. However, as far as the main themes are concerned, they overlap each other in the presented framework and agree on all major points.

IT IS A DIVINE PLAN!

Each of these schools of the Tradition presents the same information, but using at times different terms, which are not always easy to decode! Yet, they generally share the same structure, in particular:

- PLAN OF INVOLUTION—or descent—INTO MATTER and
- PLAN OF EVOLUTION— or ascent—TOWARD SPIRIT

That is why we shall call it a 'DIVINE PLAN', as it is effectively impossible for any human brain to conceive such a plan.

And, it is good to remember that if the scenario of this immense theater play has been written before the dawn of time, with its decor and lights having apparently already been decided; neither the costumes, nor the actors, nor the details of how it will be played and interpreted, have been written in advance. This precision is for those who think that we have no freedom in this great Plan! We have a lot of freedom, but it is inscribed in an immensity that does not belong to us, as it is beyond our human scope.

Preface

CLARIFICATION OF THE TERM 'RACE'

This synoptic table of the SEVEN RACES requires a clarification and an explanation of the term 'race', written here deliberately in capital letters. It is to make a distinction between these seven great Humanities or seven RACES, and the term 'race' as we use it today for different skin colors and other characteristics.

Moreover, a great RACE—sometimes called 'Mother-Race' or 'Root-Race'—contains at times the four skin colors (example: 4th and 5th RACES, the only ones that a memory or a reading is sufficiently accessible by the great spirits who have developed their spiritual abilities).

Furthermore, the term 'Aryan' (also called Caucasian and post-Atlantean) used for our 5th RACE must be redefined in the context of the initiatic tradition. If Hitler used the term in his Machiavellian plan, it is because he used esoteric notions reversing their values, distorting them for his own profit and putting them at the service of destructive forces. This is obviously not our goal here, nor was it in the initiatic science!

A FEW MORE PRELIMINARY OBSERVATIONS

What is the 'Akasha Chronica'?

According to the Tradition or initiatic science, all of the true 'History of Humanity' is inscribed in the Akasha Chronica (also called Akashic Records). It is the etheric memory of the Universe that can never be erased, unlike that of humans, who can hide or reveal it according to the epoch and according to their sole interest.

Only those who have developed authentic spiritual faculties since time immemorial can access the Akasha Chronica. It is not yet our case, as we only make a synthesis!

The Great Masters and Initiates, keepers of the Initiatic Tradition

They are the first intermediary Servants between Humanity and the Divinity because they fully realized their own humanity and their own inner Divinity. They can therefore bring all their wealth to others because it is real, experienced, authentic, truthful, and sincere.

They are already among the 'Superhumans' or 'Sons/Daughters of God' described further on.

Thus, they can offer new methods adapted to the time, place, conditions, and circumstances for that epoch of the planet and to what humans require to advance.

They often are the great founders of religions, the spiritual guides that humanity needs to not get lost or led astray in life. Yet, they can remain completely unknown, living in the shadow of those who are much more in the forefront of action while guiding them. These great beings then prefer to remain anonymous, and serve the Divinity more in the background and in a different way.

Their influence generally extends over a Culture, enveloping it so that the great PLAN can be achieved, but it can also go well beyond that.

They are there to show humanity its path to the light, the meaning of life, the reason for its existence on this planet and the work to be accomplished.

They often have completed their evolution but make the sacrifice to return to Earth to give an example, to be a model to follow, even at the cost of their own life.

The greater they are and the heavier their burden, which is unknown to human beings, the more humble and accessible they are, always presenting themselves as such even at the risk of being considered ordinary beings, which doesn't matter to them.

They never say who they are. In reality they are immense beings, responsible for eternal and immortal duties that are often beyond them, but they are here to accomplish them at any cost.

They will let those closest to them guess it through their intuition, if that is their wish, but they themselves answer only to Cosmic Intelligence. They know who they work for.

They already know they will be misunderstood in their own time, and they have accepted that fact. In bringing lofty ideals for the epoch, and in serving the expansion of consciousness, they upset the current traditions.

They therefore shake up the established order for the purpose of advancing consciousness, but always in line with the cosmic laws to which they themselves are subject in the first place. And they also, generally, respect the human laws given or imposed in the time and place of their chosen incarnation.

The moral aspect is the most developed among them, as it is of primary importance for them.

One can be gifted, a genius, possess talents and even spiritual abilities, but it means nothing to these great Masters if the moral aspect does not govern these gifts, if it is not above these gifts and at its service. For them it is a primordial condition to know how to accomplish this work of obedience to the great DIVINE PLAN, as they themselves have done for so long!

The great Masters are foremost disinterested beings; it is their principal quality and virtue. Their focus is to work on themselves, to be masters of themselves in the noblest sense, and to serve the great cause for which they came. The only role that suits them is to be useful to human beings of their epoch, in agreement with the universe and with the cosmos; and for that, they will sacrifice everything. For their vision is large and broad, it embraces immensity and the great unfolding of the human consciousness through eternity. They hold no narrow-mindedness within themselves, no limiting beliefs, no bigotry.

They only obey this inner Being that guides them from within, for they have successfully passed through numerous initiations in the temples or pyramids of various eras, countries, and continents.

They have given proof of their elevation and their desire to serve humanity to those who surpass them, and to whom they answer for their work.

This is what makes for their greatness, inner depth and originality, for they are all different and speak with their uniqueness, their own structure, language and experience.

Yet, the common principle they all share, and that unites them all, is the fact that they humbly submit to the DIVINE PLAN which they know, honor, understand and which makes them accept everything with patience.

The past, present, and future of humanity *are* revealed to them.

In their great compassion, they are aware that the human beings they instruct are far from their state of consciousness, and it requires all their love to raise them towards the Light. Equally, it requires all the love and trust of those who decide to follow them, to walk with them and to serve them; not for their own gain but rather to move forward in this great living theater, on the stage of the planet Earth, itself connected to the cosmos!

Heirs of the initiatic tradition throughout the different deluges, they have sought and found it thanks to their highly developed spiritual faculties, and due to the relentless work they have done on themselves with perseverance and constancy, overcoming all the obstacles they encountered on their path.

They are our 'Older Great Brothers' who know how to travel safely on the path ahead, and how to overcome every danger by the inner light that always abides in them.

We can trust and follow them, for they do not mislead us.

Therefore, they did not devise a story of our past solely through their intellect, such as is the case with official history books. By limiting the great 'History of Humanity' to only a short segment of time, humans, who live on Earth unconsciously, do not indeed have an awareness of the numerous factors that would allow them to develop a great respect for 'their Mother, the Earth'. Thus they could also respect its Creator with his Creation and his Creatures.

Fortunately, the time has now come to lift the veil. And the conditions to know, understand and study are now possible; accessible for all those who desire it, who are on an inner quest. The urgency is evident all around us.

AN IMMENSE PUZZLE ASSEMBLED IN ORDER TO BE USEFUL

The information assembled here contains pieces of an immense puzzle that sincere and passionate seekers can attempt to put together—if they so desire—to achieve the best conclusion possible, one closest to reality, most accurate, precise, honest and stringent, according to each one's ability. They can then attempt the same research as us yet arrive at possibly different details in the end.

Of course, all of this is based on intellectual research, but not only, otherwise it would not have really interested or motivated us!

Passion stimulates and vivifies research.

The desire to finally see more clearly and position ourselves in relation to a PLAN that surpasses us, fulfills us, is our primary motivation.

Intuition and the love of assembling the dispersed pieces of knowledge make up the rest.

Yet another driving force is the wish to be useful, so that others may understand this topic as well.

Although the main points that came to mind have been better defined—perhaps we still forgot some—we are also aware that many notions still elude us. So we ask for your understanding and indulgence, despite all the work and decades of research.

Astrological SIGNS		DATING Characteristics	THE
		Humans live within God They are androgynous	Inv
		350 000 000 years	2ᵣ
		Bone system solidifies The 5 senses are forming Still androgynous	"
		3 000 000 years	3rᵈ
		1st PHYSICAL RACE **Separation of soul mates** Loss of androgynous state, the 2 sexes appear Beginning of successive reincarnations	Fev
			CATACLYSM BY EART
		1 000 000 years	4th RAᶜ
		7 Cultures	1st Culture -
			2nd Culture -
		Culminating Point of the RACE ⟶	3rd Culture -
			4th Culture -
		Stem of the 5th RACE ⟶	5th Culture -
			6th Culture -
			7th Culture -
Virgo		12 960 BCE	
		10 800 BCE	CATACLYSM BY WAT
Leo		8 640 BCE	10 000 years	5th Rᵉ
Cancer			
Gemini		6 480 BCE	7 Cultures
		4 320 BCE	Approximate dates	1st Culture -
Taurus		2 160 BCE	2nd Culture -
Aries			3rd Culture -
		0	4th Culture -
		Beginning of Evolution	We are here ⟶	5th Culture -
Pisces		2 160	End of 5th Culture	6th Culture -
Aquarius		4 320	7th Culture -
Capricorn		5 709 End of 5th RACE (Baba Vanga)	
			CATACLYSM BY Fi
		It shall be a Solar RACE	☼
			(Emaᵣ
		Humans will reincarnate on their own	
		Fusion with the Divine **Inner fusion with soul mates** Sexual organs disappear	
			END OF EVO
		Humans will leave the planet to	

INVOLUTION

EVOLUTION

ES ON EARTH	PLAN
- POLARIAN	NON INCARNATED
e an etheric sphere	
	SPIRIT- GROUP consciousness
HYPERBOREAN	UNIVERSAL and DIVINE
ea or Thule	
End of Paradise	End of Buddhic consciousness
EMURIAN (Black)	INCARNATED CONSCIOUSNESS
GIANTS	Development of instinct,
er Island, cyclopean	feelings - instinctive vision
/ Pacific Islands)	

- Volcanic eruptions. Lemuria sank into the Pacific Ocean

EAN (Red dominance)	
ed giants)	Consciousness of the EGO (Me)
wn red)	Development of Self-Consciousness
	Concrete thinking
ellow)	
ITES (White)	
hite) Sterile culture	
low) Sterile culture	

hers : - 50 000 - 28 000 bce (**Edgar Cayce**) - sank into Atlantic Ocean

N (White dominance)	
Europe	ANALYTICAL consciousness
US	Development of the intellect
ANS	Abstract thought
SSYRIANS - BABYLONIANS	Reason
ANS	
OPEANS	Culminating Point of the RACE
	Stem of the 6th RACE

nt of the 6th RACE shall rise from the Pacific Ocean

- LUMINOUS	
w, gold as dominant colors)	FRATERNAL consciousness
	Development of the Soul
iples	Intuition / Clairvoyance
	resting on intellectual basis

CLYSM

RACE	
	DIVINE consciousness
ters	Development of the Spirit
	Divine Creation

UMAN BEINGS ON EARTH

r little brothers / Angelic kingdom of the humanity

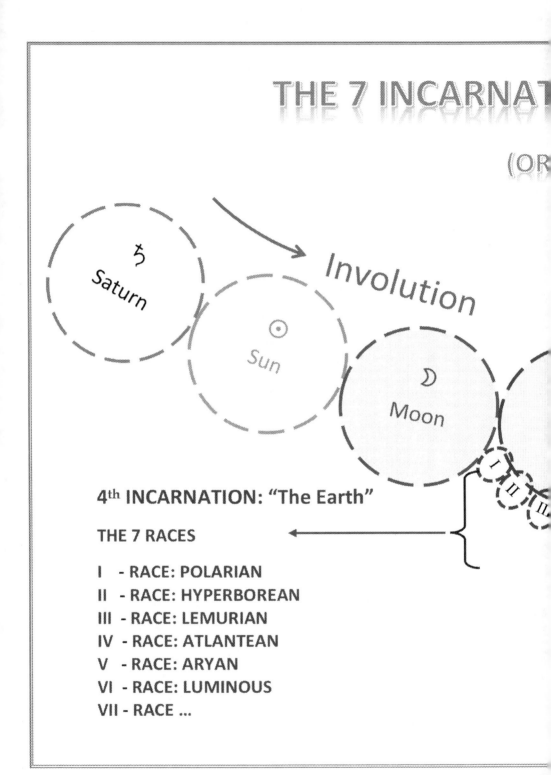

THE 7 INCARNAT

(OR

ℏ
Saturn

☉
Sun

☽
Moon

Involution

I
II
II

4ᵗʰ INCARNATION: "The Earth"

THE 7 RACES

I - RACE: POLARIAN
II - RACE: HYPERBOREAN
III - RACE: LEMURIAN
IV - RACE: ATLANTEAN
V - RACE: ARYAN
VI - RACE: LUMINOUS
VII - RACE ...

Evolution

Vulcan

♀
Venus

♃
Jupiter

VI VII

THE 7 CULTURES OF THE V RACE (5th RACE)

1 - ANCIENT HINDUS
2 - ANCIENT PERSIANS
3 - EGYPTIANS - ASSYRIANS - BABYLONIANS
4 - GREEKS - ROMANS
5 - WESTERN EUROPEANS
7 - SLAVS

Definitions of the words RACE and Culture
Their development of consciousness

Definition of a RACE

A RACE is a Great Humanity with a development of consciousness planned by Cosmic Intelligence. It nearly disappears when the time has come to make way for another RACE more suitable to adapt to the new conditions of the planet.

However, even when a new RACE has officially taken over the previous one, some stragglers, or on the contrary, the most evolved of the preceding RACE, remain among the new one for a very long time for different and opposite reasons.

The straggler souls will disappear little by little once their time has come. This explains why today some tribes still remain, like 'traces' of these vanished RACES, continuing to live according to the traditions inherited by their distant ancestors. The knowledge they transmitted from generation to generation can sometimes be a source of wisdom about Nature for our so-called civilized peoples, who have turned away from it.

Official science knows neither how to classify them, nor where they come from, nor why they are there, existing in the same time period as much more advanced civilizations. They simply complete their cycle of evolution in an era that is not really their own.

As for the more evolved souls, they will be the 'pioneers' of the new RACE and will serve to create its core, its solid base.

But Nature is not in a hurry. It does not rush to annihilate or to transmute a RACE, or to develop a new one. It happens gently, without precipitation, over millennia, tens and hundreds of millennia, and at times even more.

This program, or plan, unfolds according to the laws of the Cosmos. A human being is a marvel of precision and perfection that deserves our respect, for it requires so much intelligence and time to model and fine-tune it, and to make it aware of its real purpose.

PROJECT OF THE DEVELOPMENT OF CONSCIOUSNESS FOR A RACE

Once the plan of consciousness is launched—which is then only an idea of the invisible, subtle plane—it is about what some members of this RACE will attain in materializing it. The beginning will therefore be the opposite of what the Culminating Point of the RACE accomplished, yet in accord with the fastest advancing Culture, which will form the 'Stem of the following RACE.'

And we shall see the good acquisitions as well as all the faults, the negative aspect of the development of a Culture which has achieved a high level of realization: the 'Culminating Point of the RACE', and which also begins to program its own decline. One should not be surprised when noting these examples:

- The first RACE, non-incarnated, whose program it was to develop its physical body—which it didn't have yet—and which it gradually formed and materialized from the subtle planes.
- The fifth RACE, ours, whose program it is to develop the causal body, aiming for the higher reason it does not yet possess. Now, we observe that in the fifth Culture of Western Europe it has not yet managed to do so, as it has only developed the analytical intellect which dissects everything and provokes separations and wars. Nevertheless, it is the 'Culminating Point of the RACE'. But we don't see yet what is to come with the faculties of the approaching sixth Culture, that of the Slavs, whose knowledge will finally rest on reason, intuition, a fraternal consciousness and the capacities of the soul, which will make of it the 'Stem of the sixth RACE'.

Therefore, one should not be in a hurry for noticing apparent contractions where, in fact, Nature takes her time by going through the necessary phases required to achieve her purpose. What matters for Nature is her goal, and to achieve that is solely her concern. She alone knows the necessary stations to go through. There is no contradiction, even in a period of decadence which often is a necessary path for the transmutation of this seemingly negative situation.

Forms don't become perfect all at once; things materialize little by little and in stages.

ELEVATION OR TRANSMUTATION OF THE RACES AND CULTURES

In addition, none of the seven great RACES, nor any of the seven Cultures engendered within the RACE ever disappears completely. Some remnants of the people constituting these Cultures migrate all the time to different parts of the planet to mix with the native peoples, and they remain even throughout a time that is apparently no longer their own.

Nature takes its time over hundreds of thousands of years to transform or elevate a specific Humanity or a particular Culture, each having its own hour of glory at the time intended for it.

This great Humanity can be that of the predominantly black RACE, that of the predominantly red RACE, that of the predominantly white RACE (these last two RACES include also cultures of people with yellow skin), that of the predominantly luminous RACE, or that of the last RACE of which we know nothing, so long as we speak only of the incarnated RACES. Yet, the non-incarnated RACES also have their hour of glory at the level of consciousness planned for them!

So great is the complexity, nearly to infinity! Thus, nobody can claim to make a true analysis, let alone a correct synthesis of all these movements of so many different peoples over such a long period of time. And of course, we are no exception either!

PARALLEL EVOLUTION OF HUMANKIND AND EARTH

Planet Earth also participates in this great Plan together with its Humanities. Thus, human beings are closely associated, or linked, to the planet on which they live because it is also alive.[52] And if they are linked to the entire cosmos via the zones through which planet Earth moves

---

[52] "For the seeker of the spirit, the planet is absolutely not this dead material that science of nature presents. It is animated and impregnated with a soul and a spirit, as the human body is not simply what anatomy suggests." Rudolf Steiner, *Conferences on the Inner Earth*, 16/04/1906, p. 17 (our translation).

as it passes through the various zodiacal signs, receiving their successive influences, then how much more they receive the influence of the Earth itself, which is so much closer to them!

Human beings are not separated from their link to the Earth as they were led to believe for thousands of years. And it is very late to become aware of it now after all the damage caused by our lack of awareness toward the one who carries us like a 'Mother'.

Nature—Earth in this case, our 'Mother', the feminine formative principle—gives us indeed our physical body, formed from the four elements, which returns to Earth at the end of each incarnation.

She is the spouse of the 'Father', of Cosmic Intelligence, the masculine creative principle; the spirit that animates the physical body—the crust, so to speak—through the other subtle and invisible bodies endowed with unsuspected faculties, themselves linked to an indestructible, immortal principle.

These subtle bodies will be described further below, with both those of human beings and those of the Earth in a perfect parallel correspondence and evolution.

THE CATACLYSMS AND THEIR ROLES

At the end of each RACE, planet Earth is reshaped after a great deluge. But smaller cataclysms also strike during the development of a RACE throughout its Cultures to stop a course taken by humankind against nature.

The cataclysms are accomplished by the four elements, which seem to alternate. They serve the divine, angelic and archangelic Hierarchies who govern them. A flood can be caused by the elements: earth, water, air, or fire.

A new and clean continent is needed for the new Humanity.[53]

---

[53] "The continents present themselves like the decors of a theater scene where the drama of human evolution plays: as soon as an act is completed, the curtain falls and a new set of decors takes place. Likewise, all living beings, plants, humans, planets and suns are born, grow old and die so continents appear to later on disappear." Methody Konstantinov, *La nouvelle Culture de l'ère du Verseau* p. 63, (our translation).

EACH RACE IS GOVERNED BY A RESPONSIBLE GUIDE: THE 'MANU'

We know nothing about the first three Manus—the name originates in Hindu philosophy—responsible for the first three RACES. Those of the following four RACES and their respective Cultures seem to be known; however their divine program is hidden from human understanding as it exceeds a purely intellectual and rational comprehension.

The Manus accepted this task before the Creator in function of their long acquired evolution. They can be incarnated or not, depending on the conditions and needs of the RACE in which they are called to be present, to give it the necessary impetus.

They appear to be the archetype of the entire RACE and its seven Cultures. The Manu is a perfect Being, therefore androgynous, possessing inwardly the two principles, masculine and feminine, in a perfect balance.

Their mission is to lead the entire RACE to its planned development of consciousness.

They are only free when every straggling soul and every member of that RACE and of the seven cultures has reached the desired perfection to move toward a higher consciousness.

It may be that the Manus are in reality one and the same Being, the One spoken of in the Apocalypse of St. John as "having neither father nor mother, neither beginning nor end."

He would have been present from the beginning of the Earth's existence and would remain until its end. In India, he is known as Markande. And a Purana—an ancient Hindu sacred text—bears its name *Markandeya Purana*, in which it is written that "Markandeya lives eternally."

He would thus be the greatest eternal Initiator, that of all the great Masters of humanity, of all times and all epochs; as 'Regent of the Earth', he maintains the eternal principles and adapts them to different epochs under a new form.

All initiations come from Him, those of the Atlanteans, Egyptians, Hindus, Essenes, Saint John, etc.

In the Hindu Tradition, it is mentioned that Manu is also Melchizedek. At each epoch, Melchizedek changes name.[54]

THE PROGRAM OF DEVELOPMENT OF CONSCIOUSNESS OF EACH RACE

The purpose for the specific program of each RACE is to develop the human consciousness during present and future incarnations, through successive reincarnations.

The first RACE, not-incarnated yet, will perfect the physical body, which it does not have in the beginning, from the invisible and spiritual realms.

The second RACE, also non-incarnated, will acquire its etheric body and form the five senses.

The third RACE, the first to be materially incarnated, will develop instinct, basic sensations and a hazy clairvoyance.

The fourth RACE will become aware of its ego, its self, its feelings and concrete thinking.

The fifth RACE, ours, will mainly develop the intellect, analytical, abstract and philosophical thinking up to the point of reason [higher thinking].

The sixth RACE will concentrate on the gifts of the soul with its fraternal and collective inclinations for sharing, for universal and disinterested love, with intuition and clairvoyance.

The seventh RACE, the last one, will bring the highest development of the spirit and its power of creation in this era of evolution of the planet Earth, which ends its cycle of incarnation called 'Earth Period'.

If human beings, over the course of hundreds of thousands of years, have succeeded in developing certain faculties with a parallel moral dimension, it is also possible that they misuse their potential. Then, intelligent Nature remedies the situation by creating a new theater scene,

---

[54] Extract from lecture #1025 of Master Omraam Mikhaël Aïvanhov dated January 31, 1959.

more suitable to its development. And life begins again on a new basis in agreement with the great cosmic PLAN, but it never starts from nothing.[55]

Above all, the larger vision shows us a great Intelligence manifesting itself ceaselessly behind these successive attempts for the development of consciousness.

Indeed, some of the most advanced beings are always saved from the deluge and rebuild a new Humanity and Culture elsewhere on the planet. Humanity never comes completely to an end, nor does it get completely destroyed! There are always enough to continue life on Earth... everything is provided for by the Divine Plan.

THE SEVEN CULTURES OF A RACE

Each RACE seems to be composed of seven Cultures or Civilizations. Not all authors agree on this point, but such is the belief of those the closest and best known to us.

- Ours, the fifth RACE
- The preceding one, the fourth RACE, remains in the memory of humanity through legends or stories taken for legends or myths (such as Plato's Atlantis), from which researchers now rediscover vestiges, however as of yet without being able to challenge the official history.
- In this regard, here is an interesting enlightening point, unquestionably confirming the plan of involution and evolution which seems to contradict what we learned in school:

Unlike the generally accepted theory, humans did not descend from the apes or any other animals. Billions of

---

[55] "The intellect was useful for the fifth RACE, the soul and spirit shall be in the sixth RACE, as the heart was in the fourth RACE. God, who prepared a PLAN, prepares us to pass through specific stations. Also, the whole world will adopt these new notions. In the fifth RACE, the mystical aspect is added to the intellect without rejection. In the sixth RACE, everybody will live enthusiastically and be in a state of wonder. Only the good will be seen in everything and the intellect will no longer govern." (Master Omraam Mikhaël Aïvanhov, extract of an audio lecture dated April 20, 1969).

years ago when Earth's crust solidified, plants appeared, followed by animals and finally by humans. Evolution certainly took place from plants to humans, but it was only their forms that evolved. The human spirit descended only when a form that suited it emerged. This can be likened to a new house owner who takes possession of a house only once it has finished being built for them. It's not the house that produces the owner; they are not created by the walls of the house! They arrive from somewhere else and do not move in until the house is ready. In the same way, when the spirit found a body capable of receiving it and also the right conditions to manifest through this body, it descended from the heavenly region and, as it has done for millions of years now, it keeps descending. The evolution of forms was necessary for the involution of spirit to take place.[56]

Definition of a Culture

A Culture is a great Civilization that comes into existence, lives and expresses its distinctive characteristics within a great RACE, only to eventually disappear when its time comes, and make room for the next one.

N.B. It should be noted that what we call Cultures was named 'sub-races' by Helena P. Blavatsky. We deliberately did not choose that name—too inappropriate nowadays—preferring by far the term Cultures as given by Methody Konstantinov.

PROGRAM AND FUNCTION OF THE CULTURES

We see that the cycles repeat themselves in every major RACE. Thus, in the seven known Cultures of the two RACES for which we have a readable memory, there are always:

- The 'Culminating Point of the RACE': a Culture that dominates the others and carries its development and expression to the highest point. None other will attain its level.

---

[56] Master Omraam Mikhaël Aïvanhov, *Daily Meditation* April 24, 2019.

- The 'Stem of the following RACE': another culture which, by realizing the program of consciousness established for the entire RACE, already has the characteristics of the following RACE. And with these advanced beings, the consciousness for the future is built.
- 'A sterile Culture': at the end of a RACE. It manifests in the last Culture (fifth RACE) and in the last two Cultures (fourth RACE) where all the lagging souls of the previous Cultures reincarnate. The Divine Plan makes them all incarnate at the same time for their development. Yet, this sterile Culture does not bring anything further to the Great Humanity. It is also during this seventh Culture that a great flood occurs, nearly putting an end to the RACE and its plan for the development of consciousness to which it was intimately linked.

TRANSITION BETWEEN TWO CULTURES

The transition period can be relatively smooth and easy when there is a 'buffer' between two Cultures, or very difficult when the two cultures are consecutive. These two can indeed collide violently. Here are two examples:

- In the fourth Atlantean RACE, between the third Culture of the Toltec (Culminant point of the RACE) and the fifth Culture of the primitive Semites (Stem of the fifth Aryan RACE, ours), there is the fourth Culture of the primitive Turonian which played the role of buffer.
- In the fifth Aryan RACE, there is nothing between the Western European Culture (Culminating point of the RACE), which is ending now, and the coming sixth Culture of the Slavs (Stem of the 6th RACE) which will follow. That probably explains the chaos and turmoil we find ourselves presently in. As a matter of fact:

The 'old world', long recognized as such, wants to continue to endure despite having become obsolete and unsuitable. It is the descending current that is doomed to fail sooner or later.

The 'new world' would like to find its place but it is not yet officially recognized, since it is just seeing the day through the silent birthing pain of courageous pioneers. It is the ascending current which will be at the forefront in the future!

The two blocks of civilization thus collide violently, reflecting two seemingly antagonistic mentalities of the present. It is the 'clash of cultures'!

THE ASTROLOGICAL SIGNS ASSOCIATED WITH THE CULTURES

Each astrological sign lasts 2160 years and corresponds approximately to a Culture[57]. It also goes through three phases of 720 years each in the following order:

- The first: the mystical phase
- The second: the scientific phase
- The third: the social phase

Aquarius is coming like the spring arriving before the calendar date. The premises are already showing, but they are not yet official! The pioneers of the Age of Aquarius are here, announcing without their conscious knowing the sixth RACE. But without having the conditions of the sixth RACE fully in place, they encounter difficulties when they humbly try to establish and live in the innovative currents of Aquarius.

---

[57] "Under the influence of the astrological forces, the Cultures are replaced by new ones when, during the process of their development, they have given all their material and spiritual contribution to the individual, social, national life and to all of Humanity." Master Peter Deunov.
"The future Culture will be created from within and not from the outside. It is by the love for humanity that all the cosmic plans will be realized having its elevation as a goal. It is only then that the Peace so desired will be established among men." Master Peter Deunov.
"Aquarius must come in 200 years. Aquarius is not here yet but it can be felt already! Its emanation, its aura are here already acting on human beings, influencing them." Master Omraam Mikhaël Aïvanhov, extract from audio lecture of December 10, 1966).

Development of consciousness of the seven RACES on Earth[58]

THE EARTH, A LIVING SPIRIT IN THE IMAGE OF A HUMAN BEING

It should be noted that in the Tradition or initiatic science, the Earth is considered a living Spirit, a thinking, feeling, and acting *being*.

It is both a material and spiritual vision of the planet, and of the planetary bodies in general, and not only a material vision! Mainstream science believes to know what all the different planets of the solar system are chemically composed of, but it is a purely materialistic point of view. It doesn't consider the spiritual side to complement its viewpoint and, therefore, is greatly mistaken. It cannot understand a planet as a living being and instead considers it as a lifeless object.

Nevertheless, like human beings, the Earth also possesses a consciousness and a physical body, as well as the same subtle bodies. She reacts through them, just as we react through:

- Our physical body—the organs—through the five senses
- Our etheric body—vital body—through our sensitivity and memory
- Our astral body—the heart—through our emotions and feelings
- Our mental body—the intellect—through our thoughts
- Our causal body—the reason—through our superior ideals
- Our buddhic body—the soul—through our disinterested, universal, boundless love
- Our atmic body—the spirit—through our superior, eternal creative power.

The Earth is therefore not this rough 'material object' with which we can transgress all the laws of the universe without consequences, as taught

---

[58] "The Tradition has been transmitted in the temples for the past eighty thousand years, from flood to flood." Saint Yves d'Alveydre, *Mission des Juifs*, 1910, Vol. 1, (our translation).

"The history of humanity on Earth is not a coincidence. It is important for you to know that each step of the development is done according to the divine Providence, according to a divine Plan." Elisabeth Haich *Initiation* p. 317.

by mainstream science based on a materialistic philosophy. It is first of all a living being, animated by a Spirit who works through it.[59]

To the extent that we evolve, we help our planet evolve.

The Earth is intimately linked to us and reacts to everything we do on her and with her. Likewise, we are intimately linked to her even if we are not aware of it.

Our physical body comes from the Earth and returns to the Earth after each incarnation. But the superior subtle bodies, the soul and the spirit, are indestructible, as they are made of immortality and eternity.

And as long as traditional science does not recognize these subtle bodies, it will not understand the structure of a human being or that of a planet, and will therefore not be able to heal either human beings or the planet that our civilization, the fifth Culture of the fifth RACE, is attempting to destroy. The latter has only developed an artificial civilization in total disagreement with the laws of the universe, or of Nature, which it does not recognize.

In regarding human beings and the planet as the spiritual entities they both really are, the problems will be solved.

Of course, the materialistic vision was necessary for a time, but it only presents half the reality. The other half is now brought to humanity through the spiritual vision. The two visions together will allow for a more complete understanding of reality, and human beings will no longer be mistaken.

---

[59] "In reality, the Earth possesses the same structure as a human. A human is constituted of seven earths, namely seven bodies. Therefore the Earth we walk on is similar to our physical body and, like us, it has its subtle bodies. [The Earth is one of the organs of this great body the solar system is.]

All life developing on Earth is the work of the Spirit of the Earth, a divine spirit. The Earth thinks, lives, feels, breathes, evolves and it also influences humans beings." (Master Omraam Mikhaël Aïvanhov, audio lecture of January 4, 1964).

"The Earth is the physical body of a Great Spirit who solidified itself to its present state to provide us with the environment in which we can live and gather experiences." (Max Heindel, *Rosicrucian Cosmo Conception*).

The seven RACES

FIRST RACE: POLARIAN (NON-INCARNATED)

The Earth is not yet solidified in this very distant past; it is in a viscous state. Little by little, it will densify in solid mineral: it will form its crust, its own physical body.

Human beings do not yet have a dense body as we know it today. They resemble a luminous sphere allowing them to move. They have an ethereal body and what will become the physical body later is still soft, flexible, and supple. The physical body is still forming.

They are called 'mineral man' with a state of consciousness that minerals have, staying in place and waiting for the elements to transform them into dust through eons, their only way to evolve.

They are not yet physically incarnated but are bathing in the unconscious state that corresponds to their progress towards future materialization.

They are androgynous, meaning that both principles, masculine and feminine, reside within them.

They do not need another being to reproduce, and they are totally unaware of this act.

Their consciousness is internalized, they are not aware of the external world.

They follow the impulses of the divine Group Spirit that governs them. They are bathing in the invisible world, protected by God's universal and collective superconsciousness.

They live in the bosom of God as a child lives in the bosom of their mother, unaware of the dangers that can threaten them.

They have an innate spiritual perception because they come from these spiritual realms. They are linked to the Great Hierarchies who helped them acquire their form, and they communicate with them.

SECOND RACE: HYPERBOREAN (NON-INCARNATED)

The Earth is still a blazing globe, shaping its surface where islands emerge on a sea of fire. A vital body is added to its crust.

Likewise, human beings acquire a vital body, or etheric body, whose sensitivity resembles that of plants, the vegetable kingdom.

They are called 'vegetable man', with the subconscious state that plants have only to grow. But it is one step further from the unconscious state of the preceding mineral man.

Human beings are still not incarnated but progress in the direction of their future incarnations.

They are still androgynous, carrying both principles within. They again live in the internal consciousness of God through the Group Spirit that guides them.

They therefore live in the protective bosom of God and remain immersed in the invisible world, with a state of consciousness close to lethargy or a dreamless sleep.

Their bone system is beginning to solidify and the five senses appear.

They are still in contact with the spiritual realms, their only reality.

And it is there, at the end of the second RACE, that what is called the 'fall of man' takes place, which really is only the end of their inner consciousness of fusion with God.

Previously, human beings did not have an individual consciousness. It is therefore the end of their privileged buddhic consciousness, the 'end of their Paradise'.

They will soon incarnate on a new plane of consciousness with organs and faculties appropriate for their evolution and the external conditions for life on Earth.

The actual earth is a part that got separated from the Sun at the end of the hyperborean epoch. Its gravitation around the Sun was different from today.

THIRD RACE: LEMURIAN (FIRST INCARNATED RACE)

As the Earth is solidifying, the body of desire or astral body is added.

But, the Earth is still subject to great upheavals such as permanent volcanic eruptions and earthquakes. Human beings settle where it is relatively calm and stable, on islands with conditions favorable to supporting life. The continent of Lemuria then covers a large part of today's Pacific and Indian oceans.

Likewise, human beings acquire the same astral body as the animals and plants that appeared before them possess.

Human beings are then called 'animal beings' with the state of consciousness specific to animals, which allows for the instinctive freedom of movement. And here again, it is another step forward.

The physical body finally materialized through the feet first, then the rest of the body appeared, and last, the head.

The five senses provided human beings with information about the external world through rather primitive sensations. Having just left the spiritual world, they are still closely connected to it through a vague, instinctive clairvoyance.

They descended from the invisible, etheric, subtle realm—where everything originates from—to the visible, material, condensed plane.

This is the first RACE that is truly physically incarnated. But at the same time, human beings lose their state of androgyny that represented a great inner force for them.

The sexual organs are formed and the androgynous beings are separated into two persons: man and woman. The two sexes are manifesting.

It is from that moment on that they will need the other principle to reproduce and will keep looking for each other, to find the 'other half'. Thus the 'half' of Adam, the first man, was not born from his rib but from 'his other half', Eve! In French rib is called 'côte' and with the accent on the e, becomes 'côté' which is 'side', and this simple accent can change the logical context right from the beginning!

This also marks the beginning of the successive incarnations for human beings.

At that point they are black Giants with a tribal consciousness, and with highly developed instincts as mythology shows (the Titans). They do not necessarily have the same morphology as ours, like the Cyclopes with a single eye, giving them the vision of both the inner and outer worlds.

The legends and myths are not tall tales. They are born and live in the collective psyche, but in reality they come from distant truths buried in the subconscious of present-day humanity.

They have been mocked and ridiculed, but without the light of initiatic science, we are unable to find their origin.

However, all those who studied the legends and traditions around the world, their folklore, stories, or ancient documents, draw the same conclusion: these legends or myths all describe memories of one or more floods and antediluvian humanities. At the beginning of the twentieth century, Nicholas Roerich, the Russian painter, explorer, archeologist, scientist, and botanist, undertook numerous expeditions and research in this regard in many countries of the world.

These Giants, whose body of desire is not yet mastered, are primarily instinctive beings with a dominating power. They use the telluric forces to fight each other, as they can harness the forces of Nature. So much so that they use them but for the wrong reasons, and through this black magic they release a great flood at the end of the RACE.

The continent of Lemuria then sinks in large portions through gigantic seismic cataclysms (volcanic eruptions and earthquakes) before the tertiary period. But other parts of this continent and their inhabitants will remain even throughout the time of Atlantis.

Remains in the Pacific Islands bear witness of this great RACE with cyclopean constructions that still exists to this day (on small, dispersed islands in the present Pacific Ocean), and imposing statues (Easter Island). Australia, Madagascar, and other parts of South America such as Tierra del Fuego are vestiges of the past.

FOURTH RACE – ATLANTEAN

This is the right moment to reshape the Earth once again, and to add a mental body to it.

The Atlantean continent was formed—for what we know—in the location of the present Atlantic Ocean, but at the beginning it covered other large regions of the world, which did not have the shape of the present continents at all.

Simultaneously, human beings acquire an intellect, or mental body, allowing for concrete thought, while their feelings take on a slightly higher form.

They are hunters and fighters.

They are called 'humans' with the self-awareness that is attributed to beings who can reflect on things for themselves.

For the first time, humans become aware of their ego, and can finally say 'I, me', which was not yet the case with the previous RACES who were immersed in a collective consciousness based in the spiritual realm. However, it is still the feeling aspect that governs this RACE, for their thoughts cannot reach beyond a certain level.

Born among the pioneers of the third Lemurian RACE, of which we do not know much, they are considered the 'Stem of the fourth RACE'. As they are the first to people this new continent, they are still Giants, with red and brown skin. But their size will diminish with the different Cultures. Meanwhile, some androgynous beings still remain throughout the early days of Atlantis.

And although the dominant skin color of the RACE is red, it also has a Culture of almost black skin color, two Cultures of white skin color, and two more of yellow skin color.

In the beginning, the physical environment of Atlantis is still composed of a thick haze. Water is not as dense as it is today because it contains more air. The sun never shines clearly, but over time the atmosphere clears up.

The power of perception of the early Atlanteans is still more centered on the inner world than on the outer one: they can see the soul, the subtle bodies of others; of the animals, plants, and stones around them. But little by little, they gradually lose contact with the invisible inner worlds, which become hazier as the outer world becomes more defined.

Their physical bodies also become smaller.

The third Culture of the Toltec, with red skin color, is the 'Culminating point of the RACE'. And the fifth Culture of the primitive Semites is the 'Stem of the fifth RACE', ours. It has a white skin color, and it is here that abstract thinking is developing. Thanks to its intellect, it becomes the forerunner of the fifth RACE.

As for the two following Cultures, they do not bring anything more to the great RACE for they are considered sterile, yet they have their purpose for the following RACE.

The Atlanteans develop a technology superior to ours with crystals and lasers to activate their boats, factories and flying ships. They are very invested in the domination of matter and they excel at it.

Unfortunately, as in Lemuria, the moral aspect does not progress at the same pace as their technological abilities, and although they bring great material improvements, they are not spared from the perils brought on by transgressing the great cosmic laws.

A war is waged between the ones who use black magic and the priests of that epoch who work with white magic, but since they are less numerous, the cataclysm cannot be avoided.

Atlantis thus experiences several deluges in the course of its history, each time decreasing the size of this once immense continent. Finally, the last remaining island, referred to by Plato in his writings, sinks irreversibly into the Atlantic Ocean.

THE CURVE OF INVOLUTION AND EVOLUTION

The four preceding RACES are part of the INVOLUTION cycle.

The three following RACES are part of the EVOLUTION cycle, which only begins at the end of the fifth Culture of the fifth RACE, meaning the period we have been living in for the past few decades.

FIFTH RACE – ARYAN, CAUCASIAN OR 'POST ATLANTEAN'

The lesson from the four first RACES is to give the new Earth a body of reason, or causal body, so it can go further in its development.

Then, human beings also receive a superior intellect, which is their causal body. They are to develop their intellect first in the area of analytical thinking, and later, in the realm of abstract, philosophical, and synthesis thinking.

Until now, they did not know how to use these faculties because the appropriate instruments were missing.

They are then called 'man of reason', with an awareness of the higher mind, already operating in the realm of the causal superconsciousness, which seeks the causes of all things, even as it is not yet completely understood.

This also requires renouncing, for a certain time, the link with the superior invisible realm which guided them for so long. They therefore forget where they come from, and their main focus remains on the exterior world which they truly discover while trying to dominate it. It is matter around them that is their sole interest. They want to study it, understand it, dominate it and make it their own.

They then forget the inner world which was so familiar to them in the first RACES. This is the condition to achieve mastery over their brain and over matter, as far as the exterior world is concerned. And as mentioned before, their conclusions remain erroneous due to the lack of appropriate spiritual vision, which they lost to develop the other aspect connected to matter.

The Aryan RACE has its roots in the fifth Culture of the fourth RACE, the primitive Semites, Stem of the fifth RACE. This fifth Culture is of white skin color, since this shall be the dominant skin color of the fifth RACE. But as with the fourth RACE, we now find all skin colors of the peoples of the former RACES.

Its program is to profoundly penetrate matter through the intellect, in order to build a solid material civilization.

Its people reincarnate under the rule of karma and not by free will.

While it pushes the degree of materialism to the point where it is today, it loses the connection with the invisible world, and even ridicules the latter. And so it ends up denying the inner world towards the end of the Culture of Western Europe. This, of course, is the 'Culminating point of the RACE' in its intellectual, technological and material development.

But it is also creating a totally artificial world, believing it is the progress of humanity. For it believes that the only possible way is to conquer people with force, with purely human laws, and with violence and coercion!

Meanwhile, another part of humanity is awakening to the realization that it is at a terrible crossroads and, as a reaction, it opens itself to the new cosmic currents.

Thus, the beginnings of the sixth Culture—that of the Slavs—are already emerging. All the most advanced souls of the preceding Cultures will incarnate in this sixth Culture. Those who have developed the faculties of the soul: the fraternal, collective and universal dimension, and the idea of sharing.

This Culture will gain their intuition and clairvoyance based on an intellectual foundation, and no longer on a vague artistic perception as in the first RACES.

This sixth Culture of the Slavs will have all the characteristics of the sixth RACE. It will emerge with the help and collaboration of the most advanced Americans and Slavs. It will be the 'Stem of the sixth RACE'. It will be joyful and happy, and music will play a large role in its development.

The seventh Culture will be the repository of all the stragglers of the preceding Cultures. They will have the opportunity to make amends and evolve before the flood—around the middle of the Age of Capricorn—which will mark the emergence of the new continent of the sixth RACE.

SIXTH RACE – LUMINOUS OR 'NEW GALILEE'

To the Earth will be added a buddhic body, that of the universal soul. Its continent will emerge from the Pacific Ocean.[60]

The human beings of the sixth RACE will equally receive these faculties of the soul, called the buddhic body.

They shall be called 'superhumans' with the state of superconsciousness of the soul.

This state corresponds to the inherent freedom of the soul, which aspires to merge, to fuse into space, the immensity of the universe. The soul absolutely needs this freedom in order to realize itself.

It shall be the RACE of disciples, as human beings will then know the laws of the universe, which they will obey willingly and voluntarily.

A new way of reincarnation will be adapted as human beings will choose to reincarnate through their own will and no longer under the sole pressure of karma.

They will primarily develop a fraternal consciousness which was so lacking in the fifth RACE, and they will consider everyone as brothers and sisters.

Intuition and listening to the Divinity within will be re-established. Their spiritual faculties of clairvoyance and clairaudience will return, and thanks to the rigorous intellectual development acquired in the previous RACE, these skills will now be mastered and rest on solid bases that everyone can verify.

The faculties of clairvoyance and clairaudience will therefore no

---

[60] "The continent of the 6th RACE will rise from the depth of the actual Pacific Ocean." Master Peter Deunov.

longer be vague, hazy or exuberant ideas perceived by mystics bordering disequilibrium.

The link with the invisible and spiritual realm will also be re-established in the individual consciousness of each human being of this time.

The moral aspect will be largely developed within everyone.

This RACE will elevate the humble and weakest social classes, it will glorify women, and it will protect and defend human rights.

And the great Initiates, the great Masters will be called back to power for they have the knowledge of this Plan and of the cosmic laws in order to establish a just, harmonious society aligned with the rest of the universe.

It shall be the solar or luminous RACE, with human auras emanating violet and golden reflections, signs of a regained spirituality.

A new deluge will bring an end to this beautiful RACE to create a new theater stage for the last manifestation. With the seventh RACE the last part of the program will become realized: a complete return to the Divinity as an incarnated individual.

SEVENTH RACE

The Earth of this distant future will acquire a new body, one that corresponds to the spirit: the atmic body.

Similarly, human beings of the seventh RACE will inherit the atmic body, giving them possibilities intimately linked to the spirit; possibilities of which we do not even have an inkling today.

Human beings will then be called 'Sons and daughters of God' having regained the state of divine superconsciousness: holding the power of creation, formation, and realization within themselves.

That RACE will be the one of the Masters.

The power of creation of this RACE will affect all domains of life. Human Beings will create plants, animals, and people through the Word. In an incarnation, they will master their lives to the fullest extent, having regained all the possibilities of linking with the Divinity that they once had in the early RACES. But this time it will be with an individual consciousness of perfect mastery, balancing the inner and outer worlds, which previously was not the case.

Human beings of this seventh RACE will truly be gods: they will have realized the link with the Divine in their very cells. Again, human beings will become one with God.

They will therefore become androgynous again, however not in an unconscious manner as in the past but instead with a fully conscious, individualized awareness.

They shall be incarnated as men and women, but with the complementary principle completely developed within them. Thus, they will be rich with both polarities of life, giving them the ability to create through the larynx, associated with the power of the Word.

The sexual organs will no longer be needed for the creation of children. The male genitals will disappear first, then the female ones. The creation of children will remain but shall be done through the energetic aspect, through the highly developed subtle bodies, and through the fusion of the auras which will emanate the necessary elements to attract and materialize a child from the invisible world.

The physical body will have become such a perfected vehicle that it will obey the spirit and bring about the most beautiful external and internal achievements for mankind.

There is no doubt that the society of this seventh RACE will be a marvel of accomplishments and benefits for the evolution and perfection of all beings.

All the secrets of life shall be revealed as human beings will no longer abuse them.

And this is how the cycle of this planet—after the development of its seven RACES—called 'Period of the Earth' will come to an end.[61]

The 'Periods of the Earth' or 'Incarnations of the Earth'

DEFINITION OF A PERIOD OR INCARNATION OF THE EARTH

These are even longer time periods than the cycles of the seven RACES.

These periods have allowed the creation of the Earth over eons. In fact, they are the different incarnations of the Earth over immeasurable time

---

[61] "To leave the place to our little brothers, the animals, who in turn have also become more intelligent and evolved." (Master Omraam Mikhaël Aïvanhov).

frames, inconceivable to our small human intellect. Made of subtle matter, they are like celestial bodies in gestation.

If human beings reincarnate, so does the Earth in order to attain its perfection.

Indeed, the Divine Plan of the development of the seven RACES that we just described is still only a small part of the journey of life planned for the return to God. It represents only the 'Period of the Earth', the fourth period below and in the middle of an immense curve, after three previous incarnations of the Earth, and before three successive ones.

It is a little difficult for novices such as we were at the beginning, and still are in many respects, to not confuse the name of the Periods—bearing in addition the names of planets given by Rudolf Steiner—and particularly to make the connection with the seven RACES! But that is the way it is, it is not our invention. It is simply part of this immense PLAN conceived by the Divinity and not by human beings.

WHAT ARE THE PERIODS AND INCARNATIONS OF THE EARTH?

There again, the Tradition or initiatic science gives us the elements of these immense cycles:

1st: Period of Saturn
2nd: Period of the Sun
3rd: Period of the Moon
4th: Period of the Earth, the only one we elaborated on with its seven RACES
5th: Period of Jupiter
6th: Period of Venus
7th: Period of Vulcan

The first three Periods represent the descending phase of the curve, involution into matter.

The fourth Period represents the bottom of the curve[62], the most complete and dense materialization. It is ours.

The last three Periods represent the ascending phase of the curve, evolution toward spirit.

A VERY DISTANT FUTURE OF THE EARTH

Much time will go by before the next evolutionary cycle for the planet Earth begins.

Just as it took a long time for involution—our descent into matter—to take place, creating increasingly denser conditions for the Earth, so it will take a long time for evolution—or ascent towards the spirit—to manifest itself.

This means that after materialization, 'dematerialization' will follow, or in other words, the 'etherization' of human beings and their planet!

This is true for the manifestation of human beings, as we saw with the development of the seven RACES in a single incarnation Period of the Earth, but it is the same process for the other Periods or incarnations of the Earth.

The Jupiter Period of the Earth shall not require the presence of a physical body for human beings.

They will only incarnate in their etheric body, having lost the physical body which became useless with their newly developed faculties.

The Earth itself will also have become etheric.

The Venus Period of the Earth will see them incarnated only in their astral body, meaning without the physical or etheric body. The Earth will then be in its astral period.

The Vulcan Period of the Earth will allow them to incarnate only in the mental body, without a physical, etheric, or astral body. The Earth will also live in its mental body.

According to Anthroposophy, five more incarnations of the Earth

---

[62] "According to initiatic science, we are at the bottom of the curve. From now on, one third of humanity begins its evolution." Master Omraam Mikhaël Aïvanhov, extract from the audio lecture of July 16, 1972 entitled *Is humanity in the evolution or involution phase?*

would still follow, but there is no need to cover them here as it is quite far-reaching.

'DAY AND NIGHT OF BRAHMA OR INHALATION AND EXHALATION OF BRAHMA'

Here of course, we only covered a little part of the 'Day of Brahma' or 'Exhalation of Brahma' as the Hindu philosophy calls it—the manifestation of the creation and its creatures by the Creator! As the day exists, so does the opposite, the night: the 'Night of Brahma' or 'Inhalation of Brahma', the non-manifestation of the created world and its creatures.

Suffice for the Lord of the universe to exhale for the latter to appear. Suffice for Him to inhale for it to disappear, for nothing to exist. He rests during the 'Night of Brahma' and keeps creating during the 'Day of Brahma'.

We cannot have any idea of these eternal immensities! Our limited and temporal brains cannot conceive infinity and eternity.

It would indeed take us too far to further develop these periods and notions.

We leave those who want to make the effort to look in the reference books below—and in many other books not mentioned here, to which they can be guided if the sincerity is there—for the information needed to enlighten their path.

For, indeed, information comes to those who are sincere. No need to seek, it comes unasked. We have so often witnessed that.

RETURN TO THE DIVINE

The path back to the Divine is long—just as long as the path that diverged from it—but it is a grandiose program that we are asked to behold, so that we can, at least intellectually at first, understand and assimilate it.

Those who have a keen intuition, and who desire to work on their perfection, may sense if this development of Humanity in relation with planet Earth makes sense for them. Maybe it awakens a stirring within and resonates as an inner truth.

As for us, it gave us the opportunity to see where we are on this scale in relation to the Creator, his Creation, and his Creatures.

Moreover, we were given a structure by trying to see and understand this magnificent 'Order', this sublime architecture that underlies everything.

It is no longer chaos or coincidence that directs and governs the universe, but an immense ORDER!

Going back to the table and its dates

TWO GREAT CLAIRVOYANTS

Two great clairvoyants unanimously recognized on the planet in the 20th century are cited in the table, with whom we also associate other authors, great scholars or Initiates.

Edgar Cayce (USA 1877-1945)

In his lectures under hypnotic sleep, giving him access to the Akasha Chronica, he mentions three floods in Atlantis, each time shrinking this continent and finally reducing it to a last small island, which eventually entirely disappeared.

Walter Scott Elliot, a scholar of Theosophy, goes even further back in time with his four maps of the world. The first one dates back about a million years, with deluges even further back in time than those given by Edgar Cayce: -800,000, -200,000, -80,000 BC.

This is without a doubt why Saint Yves d'Alveydre—a great scholar and Initiate of the 19th century—affirms that we are in the sixth deluge! He too had the ability to astral travel and to read the Akasha Chronica.

Baba Vanga (Bulgaria 1911-1996)

She gave the date of 5709, which she calls the 'end of the world', apparently not being able to see the future further than the end of the fifth RACE, which nevertheless is still quite an achievement.

One should remember that the Bulgarian government used her gift of clairvoyance, and that people from around the world came to consult her.

The date she gave is fairly close to the approximate date calculated by one of the authors of the schematic table if we accept the fact that the fifth RACE will end just past the half of Capricorn.

APPROXIMATE DATES

Everything depends on the beginning dates of Pisces and of Aquarius, which can differ from one author to another.

As for Master Omraam Mikhaël Aïvanhov, he stated in 1966 that the true passage to the vernal point of Aquarius would occur in about 200 years.

Concerning the beginning of the Age of Pisces, it is nearly impossible to agree on a precise date, as all authors give different information.

Considering that Jesus was not born in the year 0 (but rather -6), and not on December 25 (but in March), and with passing from the Julian calendar to the Gregorian one, we still agreed for Pisces to begin around the year 0, as accepted nowadays; but we know it is an approximation!

Thus, the beginning of Aquarius would then be around 2154! And the end of Aquarius would be around 4314 (2154 + 2160 for a zodiacal year).

And we find ourselves indeed slightly past the half of Capricorn: 5709 – 4314 = 1395.

But with this Divine Plan, which encompasses millions if not billions of years, we are not that far off. Time is only an earthly notion invented by the human intellect so that people can orient themselves by means of their mind.

Conclusion

VISION OF THE GOAL AND MEANING OF LIFE

Indeed, we saw that time does not seem to count for Cosmic Intelligence, or for its children to progress, to know themselves and to finally reconnect with it one day!

For this seems to be the only true goal, the only objective and the true meaning of our life on Earth, according to all this information coming from the depths of ages and times immemorial, giving us at last A VISION.

Biography of Annie Collet and Olivier Picard

Annie Collet:

Born in France, her life has been based on two main threads anchored in the mental plane since the age of 5. They have been the guiding themes of her life, like a repeating mantra, a benevolent injunction.

1ST THREAD: 'GOING THROUGH THE ARTS FIRST'

Fine Arts studies, art professor at the "Éducation Nationale" (college, technical college program, professional high school institute).

Meeting a great living Master, Omraam Mikhaël Aïvanhov, who brought answers to her quest for a spiritual teaching and the meaning of life, in logical connection with art and her ideal.

Secretary to Prosveta Editions in Fréjus, France, who publishes the books of the teaching of that Master.

Surveillance inspector of the National Museums at the Musée d'Orsay in Paris.

Responsible for several exhibitions and theater plays in the context of an association (1901 law) or at the Musée d'Orsay. She also participated in many creations to support artists of all professions (painters, writers, musicians, actors, photographers, etc.) by designing the costumes, flyers, programs, story illustrations, theater decor, etc.

That was the first thread realized.

2ND THREAD: 'SOMETHING ABOUT POLITICS NEXT'

This thread made her rebel and put in question this rather complex notion. What could she understand at 10, 15, 20, 30, 40 years old? Nothing much!

Retired and free, her passion has been renewed with a greater depth for this Teaching that she likes so much and tries to live by at her own small level. She thought she liked drawing and painting better! But "God's plans are unfathomable" and it was decided otherwise.

Some subjects had been left waiting—despite her attraction for them—whether it was due to lack of time, maturity, and or understanding. It is through writing that new paths were revealed and above all through an understanding of inner realization at the very core of her cells.

This is precisely when she was asked to write this chapter with the help of a friend who shares the same passion. To be followed maybe in the next life...

Olivier Picard:

After being a construction worker for over twenty years, I began offering professional skills training to adults.

All along, for the past twenty years, I have developed a passion for astrology, particularly ancient astrology and it is while exchanging with Annie on her compilation work and inspiring analysis that I have embraced the study of human history. I have since dedicated seven years of my life to this vast and infinite subject.

Bibliography:

There are many more, as the subject matter is endless. But here are the main ones in chronological order:

Vasishtha and Vyasa (Hindu Sages from thousands of years ago, Vasishtha preceding Vyasa).
The Puranas, ancient Hindu texts consisting of 18 sacred books dedicated to the glory of Brahma, Vishnu and Shiva. They are older than the four Vedas written by Vyasa.
Plato (4th century BC)
Timaeus, unfinished.
Antoine Fabre d'Olivet
Lettres à Sophie sur l'Histoire, 1801, 2 volumes.
Histoire philosophique du genre humain, 1910, 2 volumes.
Alexandre Saint Yves d'Alveydre
Mission of the Jews. English Edition 2019. Original French edition, 1884, 2 volumes.
La mission de l'Inde en Europe. La mission de l'Europe en Asie. La question du Mahatma et sa solution 1901 (1 single copy remaining but republished in 1910 by Papus, from les 'Amis de Saint-Yves').

Helena P. Blavatsky

The Secret Doctrine – Anthropogenesis, 1888, 2rd volume.

Edouard Schuré

The Great Initiates: a Study of the Secret of the History of Religions, Life of Rama, Krishna, Hermes, Moses, Orpheus, Pythagoras, Plato, Jesus, French edition 1889, p. 33: introduction on the esoteric doctrine.

Sri Yuktesvar (Indian Master of Yogananda)

The Holy Science, 1894.

Phylos (pseudonym of Frederik S. Olivier)

A Dweller on Two Planets, 1896.

Rudolf Steiner

Lectures on the interior of the earth, 1906-1909 (in German), 2016 (in French), comments by V.S. Zielonka and T. Meyer. In English: *The Interior of the Earth: An Esoteric Study of the Subterranean Spheres*.

Max Heindel

The Rosicrucian Cosmogony, French edition 1909, (chap. XII pp. 261-303 and chap. XIV pp. 320-330).

Walter Scott Elliot

The story of Atlantis: A Geographical, Historical and Ethnological Sketch Illustrated by Four Maps of the World's Configuration at Different Periods, 1896 (the most ancient map shows the continents a million years ago and their evolution through the floods until the last one some 10,000-12,000 years).

Peter Deunov (Bulgarian Master)

In the Kingdom of Living Nature (under the spiritual name of Beinsa Douno), 2000, in English.

Methody Konstantinov (disciple of Master Peter Deunov)

La nouvelle Culture de l'ère du Verseau French edition, 1963, pp. 49-88, chap. 'The Races and their historical role' and pp. 268-272, chap. 'The XXth century, period of liquidation and transition between two cultures.'

L'astrologie mondiale, 1968.

Edgar Cayce

Edgar Cayce on Atlantis, 1988.

Peter Kolosimo

Timeless Earth, 1964.

Robert Charroux

Forgotten Worlds; Scientific Secrets of the Ancients and Their Warning for Our Time, 1973.

Anonymous

Les maîtres ayant fait leur évolution écrivent le livre de vie, 1983, French, p. 51 à 58.

Lytle W. Robinson

Edgar Cayce, Origin and Destiny of Man, 2008.

Jean Carigand

L'histoire liée au Cosmos, 1981.

Dorothée Koechlin de Bizemont

L'univers d'Edgar Cayce, 1985.

Elisabeth Haich

Initiation, 1960, pp. 258-267 chap. entitled: 'The Epochs of the world.'

Omraam Mikhaël Aïvanhov (disciple of Master Peter Deunov, French Master originally from Bulgaria)

The Fruits of the Tree of Life, Complete Works, 1989, vol. 32, chap. 20: 'The Land of the Living,' pp. 265-273.

The Zodiac, Key to Man and to the Universe, Izvor #220, 1986 chap. 7: 'The Leo-Aquarius Axis,' pp. 99-116.

The three astrological themes, French audio lecture of Dec. 10, 1966.

In the sixth race, everybody will manifest their soul and spirit, French audio lecture of April 20, 1969.

The different Races. Reincarnation. The Sixth Race, French audio lecture of March 20, 1970.

Is humanity on the evolution or involution path, French audio lecture of July 16, 1972.

W.H. Church

The lives of Edgar Cayce, 1996

Radu Cinamar

Inside the Earth: The Second Tunnel (Transylvania Series, book 5, 2017).

CHAPTER 5

THE IMPORTANCE OF PRENATAL LIFE FOR THE FUTURE OF HUMAN CIVILIZATION

by
Carla Machado

Master Omraam Mikhaël Aïvanhov has taught many important exercises and given a plethora of keys to inner development. And one of these keys refers to helping bring forth a new humanity, free from selfishness, madness, diseases and crimes. It is the primal period—the time spent in the womb—that is paramount in shaping the brain, the physiology and the character of a future adult, and consequently the values and conduct of a new society. Pregnant women cannot do this alone; they need the support of society at large, and as an Aquarian, born on February 17, I have signed up for that undertaking with great enthusiasm.

My adventure with the prenatal universe began when I was 24. An astrological chart reading fascinated me; it revealed so much about my inner nature in such a subtle and strong way that I decided to study this magical language: astrology. What a powerful tool! As the calculation of a birth chart considers the exact moment of the first breath, it led me to realize the importance of the precise moment one is born, our soul's choice related to what we came to learn in this incarnation. How could this choice come to be respected all over the world so that everyone might benefit from the help of the cosmos, thus avoiding misfortunes and consciously inviting the next steps in their evolution?

Five years later I became pregnant with my first child. It was a conscious conception, and right after seeing the two blue lines on the pregnancy test: "Yes Baby", I started reading the seminal book *The Secret Life of the Unborn Child* by Canadian psychiatrist Thomas Verny, one of the fathers of prenatal psychology. What a balm to my soul to read what I already knew deep in my heart, that during pregnancy, a mother can consciously help build her baby's body and psyche, improving this "construction" with her joy, her love, and good nutrition. I practiced this with my first baby, Sabrina, now a grown woman, such a wonderful creation of God. At that time I worked for IBM, dealing with Excel spreadsheets and their myriad numbers. Funny how I never did this kind of work before or after being pregnant with her. Somehow it was a path for her, for her mental development: her mind is focused and sharp, and she is graduating in computer engineering. Not a coincidence. And of course, she developed plenty of artistic talents, too. It's beautiful to see how each seed grows and blossoms in its own time when properly nurtured and reassured.

Giving birth to Sabrina and breastfeeding her completely changed my take on life. I quit working at IBM in order to spend more time with her. After dedicating so much time to my new 'project-baby,' how could I send her to day care? I wanted to continue raising her very close to me and became a mom in the full meaning of the word. I also started working as an astrologer and psychotherapist, and once in a while I volunteered in conscious birth events (at the time nobody talked about prenatal psychology in Brazil), but I always felt there was a missing piece. It was at a conscious birth conference where I volunteered as a hostess, introducing the speakers, that I met Laura Uplinger, one of the presenters. She mentioned in her speech the ideas of Master Omraam Mikhaël Aïvanhov, inspired by the book *Education Begins Before Birth*, and I knew I had finally found my life's purpose: to promote the importance of prenatal life for the advent of a better society!

Some years went by and I was expecting another baby, using the concept of spiritual galvanoplasty[63] and a lot of meditation with the sun. My son

---

[63] Spiritual galvanoplasty is the chemical process of gold-plating as an analogy to describe how the quality of a pregnant woman's thoughts and feelings can influence the development of the child in her womb.

was born at home, healthy, strong and…blond! As both my husband and I have black hair, the boy's blondness kind of shocked our families, but deep inside I knew it was a confirmation of my sunrise meditations during pregnancy. When he was three, he confirmed this inner knowing by telling me: "Look, Mom, my hair is golden like the sunrays!"

Then came another big change in my life, when the four of us moved to São Paulo so Sabrina could attend a Waldorf school, there being no Waldorf grade schools in Rio de Janeiro at that time. This move connected me to a group of people interested in promoting the importance of natural and conscious pregnancy and childbirth. In 2009, during an Association of Pre- and Perinatal Psychology and Health (APPPAH) congress in Monterey, California, a friend suggested that I create a branch of National Association for Prenatal Education (ANEP) in Brazil. I asked for a dream, as this would be a big commitment, and my husband and I were contemplating having a third child. I dreamt that Master Omraam was lying in my bed between my husband and me. He woke up, got up, went to stand at the foot of the bed, looking straight into my eyes, and I suddenly knew what I had to do.

In April 2010, we—a group of nine brave and enthusiastic women—founded this association in Brazil. In December of that same year, we announced it to potential members at the International Birth Conference in Brasilia, organized by the Brazilian Network for the Humanization of Birth (ReHuNa). During this event we realized how many people were willing to support the ideal of conscious pregnancy but lacked information about this field of knowledge. We gathered some thirty-five new members who encouraged us to devise a training course, as in those days there was nothing of the kind in Brazil. Since 1998, I had attended many conferences, met influential birth professionals, accompanied dozens of pregnant patients in my psychotherapy practice and read many books about the subject. I felt enthusiastic about the idea and sensed that our group was mature enough to start an educational program to inform people about the importance of prenatal life, helping them to be able to inform others about it and 'spreading the news.'

We conceived a program that would invite the trainees to think about the beginning of life as something huge, immense, encompassing many dimensions of the human being: biological, anthropological, psychological, political and spiritual…a program destined to inspire people not only to make a difference in their own lives but also to change the world, thanks to this new perspective.

At the start, ANEP's training course consisted of twelve interdisciplinary and transdisciplinary weekend modules (from Friday afternoon to Sunday morning), open to all who were interested. It is hard to define a target audience when the subject is life itself and should be of interest to each and every one who was ever born! We were in the town of São Paulo, the biggest Latin American business center, with over eleven million inhabitants, including the peripheral suburbs. The modules took place every three months because although the framework was already designed, we needed time to organize each module (for example, which speakers to invite), sensing the needs and receptivity of the trainees and which sub-themes they were willing to explore. We wanted the curriculum to be like a flowing river, alive and meaningful. It was (and still is) an interesting challenge, how to avoid being too didactic or imposing too narrow a point of view. And also how to honor the 'royalty' of the incoming babies and to address the abysmal lack of information about this issue, which is the main reason we created the course.

Also, I enjoyed spending time with my children and chose to be free to do so, instead of busying myself too much with ANEP's demands.

We found an amazing place to hold this first version of the course: 'Casa Angela,' a nice birthing center[64], Waldorf inspired, located in a very poor region of São Paulo, part of the 'Monte Azul' Project and the world's biggest Anthroposophical social enterprise. At the time, the center was not open for births, only for pre- and postnatal consultations, due to bureaucracies in a country with one of the highest cesarean rates on the planet. It was a fruitful partnership: we exchanged the privilege of having the course at their place for free registrations for their nurse midwives. This training course ended in 2013, and soon afterwards, Casa Angela was finally re-opened for births. Perhaps we brought them some luck?

Also, Laura Uplinger (ANEP Brazil's vice-president) and I devised a 'pocket' version of the training course and currently travel the country with this one-weekend seminar, taking the fundamentals of prenatal science and psychology to small groups interested in furthering their understanding of

---

[64] www.casaangela.com.br.

the power of conscious pregnancy for the future of humanity. We named this seminar 'Pro Mundo Nascer Feliz,' For the World to be Born Happy.[65]

In 2015, after a successful session of this seminar in Rio de Janeiro, we decided to have the next training course in that idyllic city, my hometown. As my children were older and the program had grown more 'mature,' we could shrink the training's duration by half—one module per month with a slightly increased teaching load. This renewed format with fourteen modules spread over one and a half years is the one we have been following since then, and to this day eighty-eight people have 'graduated' from ANEP Brazil's Training Course.

I believe and hope that the contents of this course can serve as an inspiration for all those who wish to create something similar in their own countries, so I gladly share here the main structure of what we have devised. The course gets updated in each group we train.

First Module

The first module is on *Sexuality - A New Perspective on Sexual Education,* and its purpose is to provide adolescents with meaningful information.

At school, teenagers learn mathematics, grammar, history, geography, but nothing about the importance of becoming a mother or a father! Sexual education classes only cover STI's and how NOT to get pregnant—no mention of loving, healthy, fulfilling relationships and the importance of inter-generational bonding.

What if we could convey to the young the idea that having a BABY, in the future, can become an important LIFE PROJECT, a way to change the world? How do they think great people, Masters and Initiates were born? Each of the great ones have amazing conception and birth stories! From this perspective, we could help to reduce the rates of big societal issues like teenage pregnancies, and improve many babies' lives with parents who are more mature.

In this module we introduce the trainees to two beautiful workshops, one for girls and the other for boys, created when my daughter was in 6th grade. The girls' workshop, "From Mother to Daughter," is a gentle

---

[65] Echoing the title of a Brazilian song celebrating the birth of a new day.

meeting woven into the Russian fairy tale *Vassilissa the Beautiful and Baba Yaga* designed to foster complicity and connection between mother and daughter. This allows both of them to trust the life values the girl receives while growing up and with which she can blossom with joy and inner safety into womanhood.

In the boys' workshop, "Passing the Torch," fathers and sons go to a place in nature near a welcoming family house. At night, each boy receives a wooden torch from his father, and with this *magical wand* in hand, faces outdoor challenges, deals with his own fears— hopefully overcoming them, strengthened by the power received from his father—and grows in self-trust. When becoming a man, conquering fear is one of the biggest issues to be faced. This is an essential step in building self-esteem and maturity in order to enter adulthood capable of embracing the important role of fatherhood, so lacking in our societies.

A strong point of ANEP Brazil's training is the contribution of special guests (at times more than one per module). We select these guests according to prenatal education's core principles and have thought-provoking lectures and discussions which coax the trainees to broaden their minds and to sense what resonates within them. The goal is for the knowledge conveyed to promote a deep-seated understanding of how relevant life in the womb is for the future of our world.

Second Module

In the second module, *Pre-Conception & Masculine and Feminine Power*, we invite speakers who are knowledgeable about polarities and the tenets of initiatic science. In Rio de Janeiro, we had a Taoist teacher, and in São Paulo a practitioner of traditional Chinese medicine. Both taught about yin and yang, elucidating those body centers (glands and chakras) through which a woman is *receptive* or *emissive* in the realm of her energies, and what happens when the relationships among these centers are based on love, trust and mutual support. Men, as fathers, are a major key to the well-being of pregnant women and their babies.

In this module we encourage the trainees (mainly women) to bring their partners, as it offers inspiring ways to prepare couples to conceive.

We conduct an eye-contact experience, preferentially between couples, but it can also be between two women, as there are few men in our classes, most of whom come to accompany their wives or girlfriends. Then, each pair receives in their hands a small amount of clay and together they model it into the shape of a nest, with the feeling emanating from their hearts.

We also encourage the couples to write an *invitation letter* for their possible future baby, stating who they are, how they think and what they have to offer, much like on a dating website. This helps them to connect with their own values and qualities, and to start preparing for a soul to join them on planet Earth!

Third Module

The third module, *Conscious Conception*, is perhaps the most important of the whole course, because it brings up the importance of creating consciousness around the baby's CONCEPTION. It doesn't come as a surprise that the theme of conception is such a taboo in societies around the world—there is little written material about it, both in sacred scriptures and in psychology texts. I believe this lack of information is due to the POWER of such a momentous event: depending on how a couple makes love. Whether attracted to each other or not, whether inspired by mutual love and admiration or not, they invite a different kind of soul. And the potent *fractal* created at conception not only impacts the life of this new being, but also the whole family and society. A single human being can be a source of inspiration for thousands or responsible for the demise of many, as often seen in tragedies.

A tool we use in this module is a brainstorming session about possible reasons to conceive a child. On an easel sheet, the group lists noble, healthy and selfless reasons to have a baby, reasons that respect the baby's point of view. And on another easel sheet, the group lists selfish reasons, fulfilling the parents' needs or those of the family (to work in the family business, be a friend to an older brother, or even to replace a dead sibling).

For the majority of the trainees, this is the first time they have thought about this theme, and the discussion opens their hearts and minds to the importance of choosing not only a good moment to conceive, but also favorable atmospheric conditions. For example, it is worth avoiding conceiving during a storm, as it disturbs the soul's electromagnetism (its frequency field), or right after an argument (the adrenaline still flows in the parents' bodies for several hours), or under the influence of alcohol and drugs (their consciousness is reduced), because the couple's *vibrations* attract a soul which echoes them.

Conception is a major key, but not a very difficult one: it involves a short moment only, and even a couple who don't often pray or meditate can pray or meditate prior to conceiving a child, harmonizing themselves in order to attract an elevated soul and thus bring a gift to the world. This is when infinity can be condensed in a second.

Fourth Module

The fourth module is *Embryogenesis & Joy,* reinforcing the importance of JOY in the formation of a robust and resilient body and psyche. Chronic stress disrupts nature's plans for perfection, tainting the image of God reflected in humankind. In this Module the trainees experience certain phases of the human embryonic and fetal life through modeling in clay. This helps them to connect with their own inner life, tracing it since their first weeks in the womb.

This is a module in which we explore the field of epigenetics, the scientific discoveries about how the prenate's environment (the mother) plays a major role in shaping his or her growth and development. Genetics are no longer understood to be the sole factor determining a prenate's health and behavior. Indeed, recent discoveries have demonstrated that although the DNA orchestrates much of a cell's functions from inside the nucleus, it constantly receives crucial information from the membrane. And this information orients the DNA to silence or activate many of its functions. Among its many roles, the membrane is in charge of reading the cell's environment, assessing it and informing the nucleus of what is going on—whether it is safe to grow, for example, or if it is preferable to enter into protection mode—thus significantly contributing to the quality of the cell's life. And the quality of our prenatal days greatly influences how we develop. The experience of it all remains stored in our implicit memory, impacting our physical and psychological health throughout life! It is beautiful to see how today's science corroborates Master Omraam's brilliant analogy between the role of the pregnant mother's inner life and what he named *spiritual galvanoplasty*. When he spoke about it toward the end of the 1930s, scientists believed in genetic determinism. More can be discovered about the fundamentals of this Module's theme in the booklet *If Three Billion Women… An Idea of Omraam Mikhaël Aïvanhov*, by Pierre Renard, and in the booklet *10 Golden Rules for Future Parents*,[66] edited by ANEP Brazil as a source of inspiration for those who are pregnant or contemplating a pregnancy.

Fifth Module

The fifth module is on *Conscious Pregnancy*, another subject seldom explored. Do people prefer to avoid this theme because of the ubiquitous clashes among pro-life and pro-choice groups? This conflict casts a shadow over the study of the importance of prenatal life and its urgently needed global dissemination… reducing this vast and consequential subject to *to be or not to be*, with the conviction that the greater our awareness of the sentient life inside the womb, the greater our reluctance to terminate a pregnancy. Understandable. We could however assign tremendous energy and resources toward educating society about conscious conception, enlisting all in the ideal that each and every conception should occur with love, and that pregnancies should receive support from the community surrounding the couple. If it takes a village to raise a child, according to the African proverb, this village should be there even before birth, supporting and inspiring the pregnant mothers. Also, society should address the importance of the first postnatal nine months, in order to fully benefit the future adult's body, mind and spirit.

In this module we offer a workshop to show how fathers can perform an *ultrasound* using only their hands and intuition, hence establishing a deep connection with the prenate through a soft touch on their partner's pregnant belly. This experience empowers the couple to sense and respond to their baby's needs with confidence, and reduces the anxiety factor that often leads to excessive prenatal tests.

---

[66] A 2008 initiative of the Hellenic Association for Prenatal Education: https://static1.squarespace.com/static/516f0a9de4b06a85f4f26f26/t/554a6fd5e4b04913fa86e360/1430941653130/10+Golden+Rules+for+parents.pdf

Sixth Module

The sixth module explores the topic of *Childbirth* and the need to respect the mother's physiology—as well as the baby's—allowing the demands of both physiologies to guide the whole process. To surrender knowingly to the power of nature is an intelligent first step toward a healthy and safe delivery.

This guidance is essential, especially in Brazil where we have one of the highest cesarean rates on Earth, possibly because a big part of the population only hears about childbirth at their first obstetric consultation, after the onset of pregnancy. The cesarean culture is strong; medical schools often allege that C-sections are the safest way to deliver (and also better suit the childbirth professionals' busy agendas), and until recently medical students were only taught the very minimum about vaginal birth.

Our birth affixes a powerful seal on our psyche and becomes our main reference for how to deal with the changes that life brings along and those we undertake on our own. A harmonious and respectful birth equips a person with self-reliance and a greater ability to embrace change harmoniously.

In this module we have a workshop in which each trainee sews a darling star doll from scratch, filled with natural wool. This helps them to connect with the energy of 'creating life' in reverence and silence, allowing for a sense of the sacred to fill the room. Such hands-on exercise deeply moves some of the trainees, and months later several share a lasting memory of this experience.

Seventh Module

The seventh module focuses on *Postpartum* and is dedicated to the quality of the baby's first weeks and months. How to minimize tribulations in this sensitive phase, when some of the mother's hormonal levels drop and others rise so significantly? We share some truly challenging cases—for example, a blind couple taking care of their newborn on their own—and this usually helps people to honor their minor difficulties.

It is also the moment when we talk about the role of the family around the couple and their brand-new baby: how to be helpful and respectful of the new family, allowing each person to occupy his or her new role—the grandparents, the in-laws, etc. The first two hours after birth are known as the *golden hours*, a hormonal window that should not be disturbed at the price of losing a natural bonding, for this period will do wonders for the mother-infant mutual recognition. We know of the importance of this moment from studying other mammals, like dogs or cats. Even ducklings, right after exiting their egg, will follow the first moving creature, considering it to be their mother, thus sometimes compromising their learning related to duck manners. Mothers who stay away from their newborn will have more difficulties breastfeeding and defending their babies as their own. Also, most babies who are not breastfed during the golden hours lose the chance to do it by instinct and will have to learn how to suckle the breast.

We have in this module a stunning photographic exhibit in homage to traditional midwives and the beauty of their work, often a lifetime devotion. In the past, they were responsible for the vast majority of births and even today are needed in the poorest faraway villages. Fortunately, their presence is slowly being requested amid the richer population and a new childbirth culture is dawning.

Another sensitive subject in this Module is death and grief, an important theme in the realm of childbirth. To talk about death helps to value life.

In this Module, the workshop includes a guided journey in which the trainees revisit their own birth and first moments of life.

Eighth Module

The eighth module is on *Breastfeeding* and how this most sacred link enlivens the mother-baby connection and fosters self-confidence in both of them.

During breastfeeding, when mother and baby are mutually enthralled, surrendering to each other's attention, love and presence, a *download* occurs from the mother's brain hemispheres into the baby's brain hemispheres.

Electronics are one of the main challenges of our times: cell phones and laptops can rob a mother's attention during what she might consider a 'boring' and repetitive action. Nevertheless, breastfeeding holds a fundamental key for bonding, and the quality of that connection will influence the child's connections with other human beings later on. Besides, a mother's breast can assess the baby's nutritional needs and adjusts the milk in order to remedy any lack of nutrients. This conveys to the baby a certainty that the world knows its needs and will always be there for him or her, an important basis for the development of faith and hope in life.

Ninth Module

The ninth module, on *Psychohistory*, deals with parenting modes throughout human history, a universe really tough to explore.

American social thinker Lloyd deMause is the founder of this new branch of history, and Australian psychologist Robin Grille skillfully interpreted it in his book *Parenting for a Peaceful World*. As we review human history, we uncover a series of holocausts against children—from murdering newborn babies as a means of birth control, to offering children as sacrifice in rituals, to abandonment and spanking (parents who didn't have enough 'courage' to chastise their sons and daughters have even hired professionals to whip them). It is painful to hear of these horrors, but it is also reassuring to see that today children are not only seen as real persons but also listened to and cared for. Of course, dreadful parental modes still subsist today and will go on existing as long as there are human beings who condone them. I hope with all my might that this madness will end very soon, as our Earth elevates her vibrations toward becoming a heavenly place.

Tenth Module

The tenth module, *Life between death and a new birth,* is essentially a mystical one. The relevance of prenatal life is seen through the scope of the amazing journey that a soul undertakes to come and incarnate on Earth.

We then invite speakers from different philosophies to present the perspective of Buddhism, Hinduism, Taoism and Anthroposophy about what the soul experiences between two lifetimes. We also introduce the trainees to Master Omraam's explanations about the afterlife, as our purpose is to convey the idea that babies bring their own experiences to this world and choose the culture in which they want or need to be born, as well as their parents.

It is a joy to see how Brazilians are not only very open to diverse spiritual perspectives but are willing to hear and discuss different understandings about the unfathomable.

Eleventh Module

The eleventh module is focused on *The First Years of Life*. Once pregnancy, birth and the first nine months of life have gone by, there is still much to bring to light: the sacredness of the first years, the importance of respecting children's nature and at the same time nurturing them with joyous and meaningful interactions, fairy tales, natural toys, rhythm and harmony.

We bring alternative points of view about healthcare, empowering the parents to let their intuition guide them and to withstand challenging moments with faith and lucidity. Small children expect to become their parents' 'Masterpiece'; they build their notion of God through this very relationship, so when parents are too insecure, their behavior might not be very helpful in creating this essential construct. Of course, this is not about being perfect parents, but learning from each mistake and striving to thrive.

Twelfth Module

The twelfth module, *Growing Up & Learning with Joy,* is devised to share with the trainees how the twelve senses develop, presented by a quite extraordinary elementary class teacher from a local Rudolf Steiner school in São Paulo.

We also talk about the importance of each parent knowing their own story, their *biography*, because every child brings back to life many memories of each phase of his or her parents' childhood, especially the child of the same gender as the parent. When we are aware of that and pay special attention to it, we can prevent future troubles, even diseases and depression, linked to how parents experienced their own early years.

There is a very joyful moment in this Module when we share outstanding, beautiful and inspiring children's books with the audience. Gorgeous stories, poetry and illustrations for little ones and stories read out loud are great educational tools for children and their parents. They add an enriching challenge for intellectual moms who were used to working hard with their minds at their previous jobs and now can learn great stories and songs by heart with their children.

Thirteenth Module

The thirteenth module, *Promoting and Inspiring Prenatal Education in Brazil and Around the World,* comprises several brainstorming sessions on how to take prenatal education to the attention of many around the globe, to people in the political, educational, religious, social and artistic arenas.

We offer a workshop on cooperative games, and some of the trainees present ideas for their projects. In the last training, as the planet was in social isolation mode, we ran this Module via Zoom and had the privilege of the participation of Dr. Thomas Verny, who shared with us some of his thoughts about how to awaken the world to pregnant women's power over our future.

Fourteenth Module

In the fourteenth and final module, the trainees are invited to prepare a presentation. According to their experience, affinities, and fields of expertise, each of them develops a project on one of the themes of the course. Most devise a project to spread to their communities using a specific aspect of what they have understood during the training.

Among many projects, we already have: a beautiful magazine about what every pregnant woman should know; the inclusion of the *10 Golden Rules for Future Parents* in the marriage preparation classes of a Catholic church near São Paulo; an autobiographical theater play; a study on epigenetics and homeopathy for childbirth; painting and star-doll workshops for pregnant women (within the context of a public health center of a Brazilian southern town); a gestational center named Harmony for Life, part of the public health system and exclusively dedicated to the well-being of pregnant women, in a picturesque little town by the sea.

Throughout these modules, Master Omraam is quoted numerous times, not only for his contributions on the subjects of conception, pregnancy, breastfeeding and the afterlife, but also for the extraordinary ways he teaches how to permeate our daily lives with spirituality. As the importance of pregnancy for the quality of human civilization is gathering momentum among couples and birth professionals, questions arise as to what a conscious pregnancy requires. For those questions, we have Master Omraam's philosophy, and in every Module we draw freely from his teachings, from the latest scientific findings, as well as from the wealth of each trainee's experience.

I hope this bird's-eye view of the modules gives you an idea of how ANEP Brazil strives to bring knowledge and inspiration to its trainees. And yes, the groups are small, but we keep in mind American cultural anthropologist Margaret Mead's saying: "Never doubt that a small group of thoughtful committed citizens can change the world; indeed, it's the only thing that ever has."

Moments of inspiration for women who wish to participate in the Golden Age[67]:

> The possibility exists, thanks to the power that nature has given to women, for the world to be peopled one day with wonderful, healthy, good and intelligent men and women. Nature has given women powers which they have not begun to exploit to the full, or which they exploit for the wrong purposes. They must be made aware of their potential and must realize that the future of the whole human race is in their hands. In spite of their intelligence and their skills, men cannot do very much in this area. It is the mother, woman, who is preordained by Nature to fashion the child in the womb.

---

[67] These quotes are from the last two chapters of *Spiritual Alchemy*, in the Complete Works Vol. 2, by Omraam Mikhaël Aïvanhov, Prosveta S.A., 1989.

And I would ask the sisters in this Teaching to have it at heart, at the very least, to enlighten all their sisters throughout the world who still know nothing of all this.

The regeneration of humanity is possible only on condition that we take care of the children...even before their birth: in other words, if we take care of pregnant women.

Instead of spending billions and billions on hospitals, prisons, magistrates, schools, I would advise the State to take care only of its pregnant women: the cost would be far less and the results would be far better. I would ask the government to acquire several hundred acres that I would choose in a very beautiful, well oriented area of the country and to plan an estate there. There would have to be residences, for which I would give some indications as to style and colours, etc. and they would be embellished with paintings and sculptures and so on. There would be parks and gardens, also, with all kinds of trees and flowers. This is where the future mothers would live during their pregnancy. The cost of their food and lodging would be borne by the State. They would spend their nine months in these beautiful, poetic surroundings, going for walks, listening to music and attending lectures about how to live the period of gestation: what to eat, of course, but also and more important, how to work by means of their thoughts and feelings on the child in their womb. Their husbands would be allowed to visit them, and they too would have to learn how to behave towards their wives. In this way, in conditions of peace and quiet and beauty, women would bring children into the world who would be fit channels for all manner of heavenly blessings.

Mothers have the potential ability to work miracles for the world: it is they who possess the key to the forces of creation. Women could transform the whole of humanity within fifty years, if only they applied the methods of spiritual galvanoplasty. And men must help the women.

Biography:

Carla Machado is a systems analyst who worked for twelve years at IBM. She changed direction in 1998 after the birth of her first child and became an astrologer, a psychotherapist, a Flower Remedy therapist and a facilitator of women's therapeutic groups, working with fairy tales and art crafts. She is the founder of ANEP Brazil and its president since 2010.

CHAPTER 6

PROGRESSING WITH THE FOUR SACRED SCIENCES

by

Dorette Chappuis

In the present chapter, we will introduce you to different means of progressing toward inner fulfillment. To begin with, we would like to point out that we referred to the teaching of Omraam Mikhaël Aïvanhov to outline this subject.

We would also like to mention that we see life as a wonderful school. The people and situations we encounter every day are all opportunities inviting us to keep progressing. The aspiration we nourish for something luminous mobilizes our energies and opens the path toward infinity and eternity. Don't they say that happiness is not the goal; it's the journey. So, let's go traveling...

In *The Way of the World*, the famous writer, photographer and traveler, Nicolas Bouvier invites people to not only discover foreign countries, but also to consider their travel as an inner quest as well. In both cases, Nicolas Bouvier explains that "some think they are taking a trip but in reality, the trip is what makes them or breaks them." In the same way, the itinerary will shape us from the very first step, be it physically or spiritually. And this journey, like any journey, begins with the first step.

Life is like an initiatic journey that should lead us step by step toward harmony, allowing both our spirit and our body to travel. All along this journey, we will experience joy but also some trials, as it is for all initiations. Life is an initiation! Seen in that light, life offers us many possibilities to strengthen our will, to develop the intelligence of our heart and the power of our thoughts.

All journeys—within or around the world—are a gateway to the unforeseen; they require an openness to change and to often leave one's comfort zone. And, this is when travellers truly begin their journey and start to integrate the transformation even without their knowing. Again, in *The Way of the World*, Nicolas Bouvier explains that the journey compels 'a kind of reduction' that brings the travellers to 'more humble proportions.' We can then conclude that, according to Bouvier's concept, the journey leads to the dissolution of the self. The self must disappear to allow the Self to come forth. This aspiration to the Self is so often unconscious, yet it is the one that moves things forward.

To experience this Self, it is necessary to have some markers that will serve as signposts indicating the work to intelligently accomplish on oneself along the path. It is indeed important to have a good understanding of things, to foster feelings and desires of such power that they will release an intense energy to fulfill a realization.

This realization is foremost a new point of departure on the natural and spiritual life which gives a meaning to all our daily activities. The final goal of these activities is to allow us to rediscover the light hidden in everything and every living being.

The markers we previously mentioned *are notably those* of knowledge, a profound knowledge of human nature that leads to the knowledge of the universe based on the correspondence between the microcosm (the human being) and the macrocosm (the universe), as written on the frontispiece of the Temple of Delphi and taken up by Socrates: *Know thyself and you shall know the universe and the gods.*

To know oneself obviously requires having the necessary tools to live and act on the physical plane, but to also obtain the proper means to live and act on the psychic, spiritual and divine planes. To this effect, Omraam Mikhaël Aïvanhov conveyed a knowledge regarding four sciences he considered as sacred:

Alchemy,
Astrology,
Magic,
Kabbalah.

These four sciences help us to manage our daily lives in the best possible way so we can overcome all the difficulties, obstacles and sufferings and experience joy, peace, and abundance.

These sciences are more than just textbook knowledge; they are a pathway that brings about stability and an inner light that leads to the understanding of the meaning of life. However, they are incomplete if they are not sustained by love. Indeed, even if these sciences are powerful in bringing light and good explanations, they should be considered with the understanding that it is the love and conviction we give them that bring strength, courage and stability in all circumstances of life. It is those that allow us to keep walking on the path with assurance, overcoming obstacles, inspiring people, and living in harmony with nature.

Before covering each of these four aspects of knowledge, we will quote an excerpt referring to them:

> Never expect me to talk to you about anything other than subjects that touch upon the new life. If you do not care for these subjects, that is too bad, you can go and find what interests you elsewhere. From me, you will always hear the same topics: the new life—how to breathe it, how to eat it, how to drink it and how to radiate it, for this what matters most, and it is the only thing that interests me. It is by living this new life that all the sacred sciences will one day be revealed to you. In the smallest acts of everyday life, you can find correspondences with the worlds of astrology, alchemy, the Kabbalah and magic. In breathing you can discover astrology; in nutrition, alchemy; in words and gestures, magic; and in your thoughts, the Kabbalah. So learn how to eat, breathe, speak and think and you will possess the foundations of the four sacred sciences. (*Daily Meditation, April 4, 2020*)

These four sciences are presented in the following manner:[68]

Alchemy	Astrology	Kabbalah	Magic
Nutrition	Breath	Thoughts	Words and gestures
Eating and drinking	Breathing	Thinking	Speaking and acting

To better understand the teaching on these four sciences given by Omraam Mikhaël Aïvanhov, we selected different excerpts from his work in which he talks about them. These passages are written in a simple and easy language which he always preferred. He did not want to use a hermetic language only understandable by a minority of readers and listeners. On the contrary, he wanted his words to touch the hearts of people and to encourage them to experience what he was talking about. People are touched by an idea, a sentence, or a word. The important thing is not to merely repeat what is being said, but to verify it within oneself, and experience it in order to live the truth of his words. Everybody advances at their own rhythm, according to their own preferences or preoccupations.

What is being presented here is like a buffet. It is up to each reader to find what corresponds to their own interests and to work with it.

Alchemy, and self-transformation

To understand alchemy, one needs to begin by understanding nutrition. It is the latter that will give us the keys to truly understand alchemy.

---

[68] The oral Teaching of Omraam Mikhaël Aïvanhov has been compiled into more than 120 books in different collections excluding brochures, DVDs or CDs. Among these books, we will refer those closely related to the ones presented in this table.
For alchemy: *True Alchemy or the Quest for Perfection,*
For astrology: *The Zodiac, Key to Man and to the Universe,*
For Kabbalah: *Angels and other Mysteries of the Tree of Life,*
For magic: *The Book of Divine Magic.*
These four books are part of the Izvor collection, a pocketbook collection by Prosveta Editions, who have several publishers throughout the world, maybe near you.
As for astrology the title *Sous le signe de l'Étoile* is from the Evera collection (in French only at present) and for the Kabbalah, there is also *The Fruits of the Tree of Life*, in the Complete Works collection, also published by Prosveta S.A.

Indeed, thanks to nutrition, it is possible to understand the process of the transformation of matter. Once this process is understood, it can be applied to other, more subtle realms such as transforming a negative state into a more positive one or again, for the transformation of the self.

> Humans eat; all creatures eat, but why? To receive energy, you will say. Yes, but because our activities have more than one purpose, if we eat it is not only to keep healthy…What do worms do? They swallow earth and then expel it. By enabling it to pass through them in this way, they aerate it and make it richer and more fertile. Well, human beings are no different as regards their food. They too eat earth, a more elaborated earth in the form of vegetables and fruit, it is earth. They absorb this earth, digest it and then expel it, and they do it again and again. But it is not only a mechanical process. As this matter enters their body, it provides them with the elements it possesses, and in return it receives something from them, from their feelings, their thoughts and their aspirations. Because of their psychic, spiritual faculties, human beings belong to a much higher level of evolution than the matter they absorb. So, by enabling it to pass through them, they transform it, enrich it and spiritualize it. (*Daily Meditation, Feb. 22, 2015*)

Alchemy is the science of transformation of matter. In the crucible, the alchemist places the prima materia, the base matter, which, initially, dies and rots down; this operation corresponds to the color black. Next, the matter is dissolved and purified and becomes white. Then come distillation and conjunction, where the matter turns red, and finally sublimation, where the color turns to gold. These operations remain obscure for many and only become clear if they are interpreted as different stages of inner life. The work alchemists perform on the matter in the crucible is, in fact, the work of regeneration disciples perform in the crucible of their own body, a work to which they must devote their entire life. The regenerated matter comes out of the crucible transformed into gold: a regenerated human being has died to their lower nature and been born to their higher. Jesus said, 'Unless a grain of wheat falls into the earth and dies, it remains just a single grain; but if it dies, it bears much fruit.' This sentence can be taken as a summary of alchemical work. (*Daily Meditation, April 10, 2009*)

Naturally, we would all like to live surrounded by people who respect, appreciate and love us. Well, this is not possible. And it is no use complaining that the world is a bad place, that heaven is cruel and that there is no justice. If we were to consult the Lord to find out his plans, he would reply that we must consider these trials as exercises, tests for us to see what we are capable of. For we do not know ourselves well yet, and we have to discover all the resources we have inside that we are not aware of possessing. Transmuting the harm that is done to us is true alchemy. Alchemists seek to obtain the philosopher's stone, but it is even more important to achieve it in our soul and heart through the union of wisdom and love which turns all base matter into gold and precious stones. (*Daily Meditation, February 11, 2013*)

Whenever you act with wisdom (light) and love (warmth), you place yourself under the authority of the spirit and gradually form within you the philosopher's stone, which transmutes all matter into gold. So you do not need to look for it anywhere other than in yourself, because there is no more powerful philosopher's stone than the spirit. Strive to achieve a state of consciousness where you feel that your spirit, your higher Self, is an immortal and eternal principle, an indestructible entity travelling through space and permeating everywhere. Then you will understand that there is nothing more important than to use this power to work on matter—your own matter— in order to purify it. Revitalize it and bring it back to life. This is true alchemy. The philosopher's stone is the spiritual quintessence that turns everything into gold, into light, first within you, but also in all the creatures around you, because everything multiplies. This is the sublime dimension of the philosopher's stone. (*Daily Meditation, June 29, 2015*)

Astrology or the revelations of the starry night

As with alchemy, astrology benefits from being studied and interpreted in all manifestations of existence. It is advisable to go beyond a theoretical study because in this way astrology becomes a living language, offering keys with which to penetrate the mysteries of life.

We could define astrology as the science that studies the influences of the planets on human beings and all living things. Yet astrology alone does not explain everything, because the quality of our aura also plays an important role in what is accepted or rejected from the planetary influences. If an aura is pure and luminous, even an influence that could be considered unfavorable becomes positive. Thus, stars incline but do not determine.

When the sky is clear at night, take a moment to contemplate the stars. Imagine that you are leaving the earth with its struggles and its tragedies and become a citizen of heaven. As you ascend into space, you will feel that your soul is deploying very subtle antennae that allow it to communicate with the most distant regions, and that He who created so many worlds has certainly peopled them with creatures far wiser, far more beautiful, and far more powerful than human beings. For when you see them arguing, bickering, and killing each other, how can you believe that it is on earth—a speck of dust in immensity—that the Creator has placed his most perfect creatures! In thinking that all these stars you are contemplating have existed for billions of years, that the intelligence that created these worlds is eternal, and that you were created in its image, you will sense that your spirit is eternal too. [69]

Respiration can reveal great mysteries to you, but only if you accompany it with some mental work. As you breathe out, think that you are expanding to the very outer limit of the universe and then, as you breathe in again you contract and withdraw into yourself, into your ego, that imperceptible point at the center of an infinite circle. Again you expand and again you contract… In this way you will discover the movement of ebb and flow which is the key to all the rhythms of the universe. When you become conscious of this movement within your own being, you enter into the harmony of the cosmos and establish a relationship between yourself and the universe for, as you breathe in, you inhale elements from space and, as you breathe out, you send out into space something of your own heart and soul. [70]

The question of destiny—whether a human being is free or subject to fate—has been discussed for many centuries, and I have rarely found the right notion about it. The mistake is to believe that all human beings without exception are affected by the same laws. If human beings are like animals who only follow their sensations, their passions, and their purely instinctive impulses, they fall under the rule of fate; everything will happen as it is written. Whereas those who are more evolved escape fate and enter the realm of providence, of grace, where light and freedom reign. The great Masters of humanity belong to this category. But the majority of human beings exist

---

[69] *Sous le signe de l'Étoile, Prosveta S.A.* (our translation)
[70] *Breathing: Spiritual dimensions and Practical applications*, brochure no 303, Prosveta S.A. Fréjus.

between the two extremes of animals and Divinities; they are more or less free, more or less bound. One must not imagine that everyone is free or that everyone is under an inexorable destiny. No, the truth is that freedom depends on the degree of evolution.[71]

Kabbalah or the Tree of Life, a symbol of inexhaustible value

The Tree of Life, kabbalistic Tree or sephirotic Tree is an image of the universe inhabited and impregnated with the divine essence.

It is a representation of the divine life circulating throughout all of creation. This representation helps to stay centered and to avoid being scattered in spiritual activities.

By working with this system, balance and harmony are gradually established and understanding deepens. Work takes place in a serene state of mind.

A study of the sephirotic Tree, the Tree of Life, affords a very clear view of the spiritual work there is to be done and is a method that can accompany you throughout your life. Follow it, and your thoughts will stop wandering aimlessly, and as you succeed in moving forward along this path, blessings will be showered upon you. Returning often to the sephirotic Tree switches on new lights each time, not only bringing you insight but also purifying, strengthening, vivifying and embellishing you. Maybe you will never understand this sacred figure perfectly and succeed even less in achieving the virtues and powers it represents, but it will act as the representation of an ideal world and always have an uplifting effect on your being. *(Daily Meditation, Jan. 20, 2010)*

---

[71] Ibid. p. 41 (our translation)

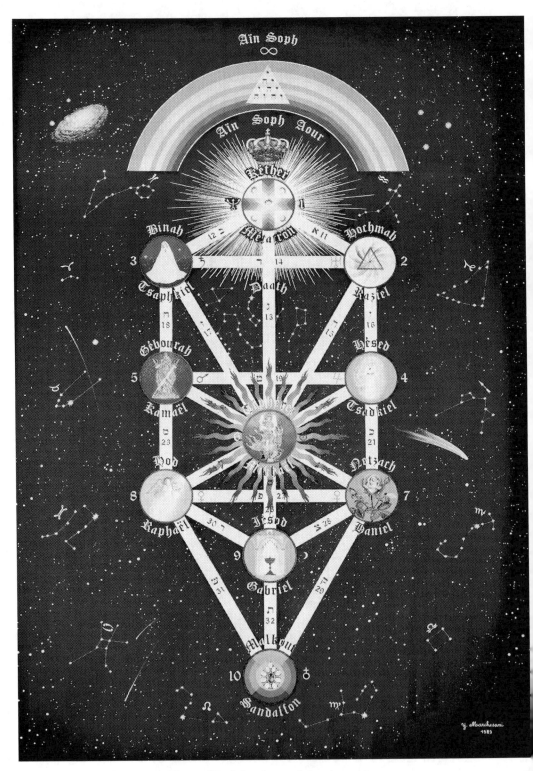

Tree of Life by Ivano Marchesani

To guide us in our spiritual work and show us which path to follow, we need a method. As I see it, the best method that exists is the study of the sephirotic Tree. Many saints and mystics have walked the path of light without knowing the sephirotic Tree, it is true, but knowing it gives a clearer view of the work to be achieved. This is why I insist that you learn to go deeper into all aspects of it. With Malkuth, you make things concrete. With Iesod, you purify them. With Hod, you understand them and express them. With Netzach, you breathe grace into them. With Tiphareth, you illumine them. With Geburah, you fight to defend them. With Chesed, you submit them to the divine order. With Binah, you give them stability. With Chockmah, you take them into universal harmony. Finally, with Kether, you place upon them the seal of eternity. *(Daily Meditation, May 25, 2011)*

Magic or the art of spreading beneficial influences

Even if they appear insignificant, all activities produce good or bad effects. Be it a thought, a feeling or a word, something is created. This leads us to the conclusion that magic is the first of the sciences. It therefore precedes the other three sciences discussed in this chapter.

The term 'magic' often displeases people. It is can be disturbing and even frightening. But when looking at it closer, we ought to recognize that even a glance belongs to the world of magic. A glance inspires joy or worry. A simple look produces an effect. How much more so with a word or a gesture?

Any activity, however insignificant it may seem—a movement, a feeling, a thought, a word—has of necessity an effect for good or bad. And so magic can be said to be first among the sciences. It only takes a movement, an influence, an imprint or a vibration to enter the sphere of magic. Each time one person affects another person or an object, they are performing an act of magic. And yet, people look, speak, think, wish, feel and gesture without realizing that all the forces they activate in doing so are magic forces. Often, they may in their ignorance set in motion negative forces which rebound on them, and when they are grasped and bitten, they do not understand what is happening to them. So it is important for everyone to learn to work on their thoughts, feelings, words, gestures and expressions, so that the forces set in motion by any physical or psychic action they perform will have only beneficial effects—beneficial for them, but also for every creature in the world. *(Daily Meditation, October 6, 2012)*

Every day, you meet a certain number of people you greet and who greet you back. If we are meant to greet each other, it is in order to do something good, to give each other something good. Those who wave or shake hands mechanically, carelessly, and remain distant and closed are making a gesture that is pointless, harmful even. So, from now on, try to be more conscious, more watchful, in the knowledge that a greeting can be a wonderfully meaningful and effective gesture, by means of which you can encourage, comfort and animate others by giving them a lot of love. A greeting should be powerful, harmonious and alive if it is to become a true communion. *(Daily Meditation, August 5, 2012)*

It is impossible to take up esoteric science without encountering, at some time or other, the subject of magic and, particularly, black magic. But it would be more sensible to leave the area of black magic alone, and above all you should avoid thinking you might fall prey to it. Those who have this fear are already attracting negative currents to themselves. Yes, because this fear makes them vulnerable and, therefore, open to all kinds of dark elements floating in the atmosphere. It's the same as with epidemics: if you are fragile and receptive, you catch every germ from people you meet, but if you are robust, resistant and emissive, you escape them. So, don't worry about black magic: make yourself strong, think of the light, work with the light, as then the light in you will repel the negative. A wheel that's turning very fast throws off the mud, but as soon as it begins to turn more slowly any dirt sticks to it. And when the flow of a spring is strong, it sweeps away the leaves and twigs that might otherwise obstruct it. So, instead of allowing your mind to become lazy, be like a spring. *(Daily Meditation, October 27, 2010)*

We leave imprints on all the objects we touch; and even if we do not touch them, our very presence, the emanations of our physical and psychic bodies are imprinted on them. And we also leave traces in the places we visit, on the people around us or those we meet. That is why it is so important to work at improving and purifying our thoughts and feelings, so as to leave traces of light everywhere.[72]

Conclusion

What we can retain from the explanation of these four initiatic sciences is that they allow us to preserve, purify, renew and sublimate life if we know how to use them consciously, with love and light.

Why setting them in relation to life? Why do they have such a pervading influence on our lives? Simply because the most insignificant acts of our daily lives are connected to these sciences as we discovered in the correspondences we mentioned.

So, in nutrition, we find alchemy; in breathing, astrology; in thinking, the Kabbalah; and in words and gestures, magic. Drinking, eating, breathing, thinking, speaking and acting—aren't those part of our daily lives? When studying in depth the law of correspondences between the microcosm and the macrocosm we can act freely on one or the other, conscious of the interrelation between these two worlds.

---

[72] Extract from the CD *Déposer des empreintes de lumière* (our translation).

A new horizon is dawning. Multiple possibilities are offered to us to become the creators of our own lives and the artisans of humanity where more respect, solidarity and peace prevail.

Biography: See Dorette's biography in her chapter 3 entitled: *Finding a Balance Between the Masculine and Feminine Principles for a Harmonious Development.*

CHAPTER 7

THE AWAKENED HUMAN BEINGS WILL BE THE 3RD TESTAMENT

by
Henriette Dufeu

Almost everyone nourishes the desire to live in harmony, peace, joy, happiness and beauty. This state of balance and this magnificent life we call the Golden Age. Can this be accomplished on Earth? Or is it just a dream, a utopia?

Yes, we can accomplish this dream and live in a world of peace. Yes, it is possible but under what conditions?

When we collectively awaken to a new consciousness and understand that solidarity, collaboration, mutual support, altruism, and cooperation are the most efficient means to make a better world.

When independently of our race or ethnicity, we understand that as human beings there are more things uniting us than separating us.

When we become aware that all of us share the same needs, be it on the physical plane: to eat, drink, sleep and procreate; on the emotional plane: to love and to be loved; on the intellectual plane: to be able to study, understand, know and to comprehend the people around us; and on the spiritual plane: to meditate, pray, contemplate, help others by enlightening and supporting them.

We will then realize all the advantages and benefits of developing a spirit of fraternity so that one day humanity will form a big family where all humans are free and have the possibility to study, perfect themselves, improve and become more useful and happier.

In his teaching, the philosopher and pedagogue Omraam Mikhaël Aïvanhov tells us that it is within us that we must first create peace before it can finally prevail on Earth. He gives us many methods and the means to work on ourselves and further develop our consciousness. He also states that "peace will only exist when our lower nature obeys our higher nature."

What are these two natures that manifest in a human being? A limited, egocentric nature focused on itself and an altruistic one focused on others, toward immensity and infinity. The egocentric nature that, although it fills the needs of the five senses, is never satisfied, and the altruistic nature that lives in plenitude although it does not possess anything material.

The lower nature is more instinctive; it only thinks of itself; its pleasures, its needs and its survival. It uses all its energies to satisfy itself even at the detriment of others. This nature is limited, egoist, personal and greedy. It wants to dominate, take, possess, get richer and always acts selfishly. This nature is linked to the physical body.

The higher nature is more generous, nobler; it wants to give, to share and to distribute its wealth. It is linked to the soul and spirit in each one of us. This nature manifests within us as love, wisdom, compassion, self-control, beauty, purity, dedication, patience, abnegation, and selflessness.

The lower nature possesses inexhaustible energy, with solid and profound roots that nourish all our instinctive behaviors, those that keep us alive. However, if it does not receive the light of the higher nature, it will waste its energies in pleasure and covetousness. Only thinking of its pleasure, to impose upon others, satisfy itself and even dominate and become violent toward others.

Our divine nature is more altruistic; it is never separated from others. It thinks above all of others' wellbeing, of the collective interest. It needs very little because its needs belong to a more spiritual nature and its manifestations are always inspired by love, sacrifice, and selflessness.

Although they appear opposite, these two natures are necessary, for they both have a purpose. It is when human beings find a balance between the two that harmony will prevail in their hearts and light in their minds.

When their lower nature is at the service of their higher nature, then peace will come within and around them.

Yes, to realize inner peace, human beings must get closer to their higher nature without eliminating the lower nature. At present, we oscillate between the two natures, at times satisfying one at the expense of the other. But if we decide to do real work on ourselves by using all the inexhaustible energies of the lower nature to feed a higher, selfless ideal for the good of others, for the collectivity and for all humanity, we would then participate in the divine work: to realize peace on Earth and to establish a harmonious relation between all beings.

Elevating our needs and developing our higher nature

In our present culture of abundance and consumerism, we are constantly pulled to acquire more material possessions, objects we do not really need but which we are led to believe are essential to our happiness. Some even go into deep debt to satisfy these illusory needs. Has this made us happier? Unfortunately, no; to the contrary, we have created more dependencies and, unknown to us, we have become more and more entrenched into this material life, neglecting the needs of our souls and spirits.

It is increasingly more difficult to understand the extent to which the lower nature governs our lives. We are so used to satisfying the least whims of this lower nature that we feel unhappy when we do not. And the more we satisfy its wishes, the more we become enslaved to them, always asking for more and the situation becomes insatiable.

Let us take the example of a smoker: in the beginning, a few cigarettes a day are enough. But after a while, it becomes impossible to do without them; and as time goes on, the desire to smoke becomes an obsession. It is an endless vicious circle that brings a temporary satisfaction but never a stable and durable happiness. So, where is the true, permanent, unwavering, and immutable happiness? It lies in the mastering of the inferior nature and in the development of the spiritual nature.

When studying the structure of the human nature, we become aware that beyond the physical body, we possess more subtle bodies: the etheric or energetic body that surrounds and protects our physical body; the astral body, center of our emotions and the mental body, associated to our intellect. On the higher plane, we are also composed of three bodies related to our spiritual nature: the causal body, the superior intelligence; the buddhic body, the soul; and the atmic body, the spirit.

To be awakened and vivified, these bodies also require a nourishment just like the physical, astral and mental bodies do. But this nourishment is made up of thoughts, feelings, looks and gestures of another nature: purer, nobler, more selfless, that free us instead of enslaving us. When we nourish these subtle bodies through meditation, prayer, contemplation, abnegation, compassion, altruism and loving kindness, we acquire peace, serenity, light, contentment and plenitude.

It is when we give priority to this divine nature within each of us that we come closer to a stable and durable happiness. It is by sublimating and mastering our egocentric nature that we free and elevate ourselves. But this does not happen overnight. We need a long practice of observing and dominating ourselves, but also nurturing a high ideal through our love and developing our willpower to resist the illusory attractions and pleasures that undermine us.

However, if we are sincere, if we work with faith, love and hope, we will become ever more the masters of our desires and of our destiny. We will notice great changes in our lives; many difficulties will slowly disappear and clarity, light, warmth, wellbeing, and happiness will increase.

Eventually, there will be no more contradictions within us and we will experience new states of consciousness, new joys that bring an incredible sense of freedom. We will discover sublime states, indescribable happiness and live in infinite spaces of beauty, joy and light.

From a personal thought to a collective thought: an extraordinary solution for developing our higher nature

Thought is an immense power given to us by Cosmic Intelligence to help us become free and approach the divine perfection that is dormant within every one of us. Everyone can develop this extraordinary faculty by becoming increasingly more conscious, by transforming ourselves and the society in which we live.

In the present era, we generally use this faculty to find ways to improve our comfort, to meet our ordinary needs and fulfill our desires. So many things are invented just to satisfy the latest innovations in various domains and bring pleasure on the physical level.

If human intelligence is capable of creating all these technological means to facilitate our existence, imagine what this unlimited power of thought can do to improve the beauty of our inner life, to amplify the good in us and around us.

How many extraordinary results we could achieve with our thoughts and our imagination if we concentrated on beauty, light, peace and harmony, and wished the best for ourselves and all living beings on Earth! If we work for a long time on these mental creations, some sensitive people will capture these thoughts and positive energy and, in turn, will wish to contribute to a better world for the future of humanity. But for this to happen, a lot of love is needed to support these divine projects, keeping faith that, with time, everything becomes possible.

Initiatic science teaches us that thoughts are living entities circulating throughout the universe and, according to the way we live, we attract those thoughts that correspond to us. They inhabit us as long as we nourish them, to help us or disrupt us according to their nature.

However, the more we elevate ourselves through meditation, contemplation and prayer, and send waves to harmonize, illuminate and embellish life around us, the more we can attract luminous entities that come to help, inspire and support us.

There are so many subjects to meditate on: harmony, beauty, intelligence, purity, happiness, gratitude, compassion, the invisible world that exists beyond us, and on the virtues, goodness, love, sacrifice, etc.

With thought we can remediate everything and neutralise all sadness, all the difficulties, as our creative power is unlimited. To verify its power in our daily lives, we can try some conclusive experiments. For example: when you are depressed, consider that this is a temporary state and try to remember all the moments of joy and happiness you have lived, and which will come again. Think also of all those around the world who live in the same state as you do presently. Send them some light and warmth saying that things will get better soon. You will notice your sorrows disappear and you will start feeling better. You will know that somewhere in the world there are those who received your good thoughts and find faith and hope again.

Some years ago, I had that extraordinary experience myself. I was rocking my sister's young children whom I had custody of after she passed away at the age of 48. Despite my sadness, I was trying to comfort them as best I could, but it was difficult because I missed her tremendously. I began thinking about all the wonderful moments we shared together, about this world of light where she now was, finally free and without suffering. I then felt a soft warmth filling me, a delicious feeling of peace. I felt her so close, right beside me, beyond the veil of things, and that she came to rock the children through me.

After a few minutes, I thought of all the children left alone in the world and who would greatly appreciate being rocked and comforted. Through my two lovely nephews, I imagined taking into my arms all these children, holding them with love and tenderness. It was magical because after a few minutes, I was no longer focused on my sadness but rather on this extraordinary work I could do by my power of thought to help others. It was such a revelation. I understood then how possible it was to act on one's own suffering by trying to alleviate the suffering of others.

At any moment, through our thoughts, we have the power to change our perception of life and give it the direction we wish for. Our creative power is unlimited. Of course, it is not always easy to realize that, as we must overcome the emotions, sadness, sorrow and pain. Yet, it is possible. Through our imagination we can console, help and support others, improve ourselves and create the favorable inner conditions to develop the virtues and qualities useful for us and all those around us. By practicing even a few minutes a day, great results can be achieved.

And since thought circulates in the subtle planes, we can link to all beings surpassing us in their development and evolution, and ask them to help us, guide us and inspire us. We can communicate with the entire universe. We can be in touch with all the living beings of the visible and invisible worlds, send light to all creatures and hope the best for each of them.

When our consciousness awakens, we will realize that we are linked to the entire universe, nature and all life. We will also understand that all our behaviors, the smallest of our gestures and all our thoughts, have an impact around us. We will then realize that imagination is an extraordinarily powerful means to create wonderful things and to participate towards an immense work of transformation of the world into a great brotherhood and sisterhood where all men and women can live in harmony, peace, love and light.

How to use all our living conditions to perfect ourselves and expand our consciousness

The expansion of consciousness plays an important role in life such as seeing the world from a different perspective and understanding with greater depth and clarity everything around us. It also offers us the ability to develop our love, tolerance, and compassion towards others, awakening in us the desire to bring them warmth, light, support, protection and assistance.

When our subtle bodies develop, we become able to feel the joy and sorrows of those around us and the feelings we awaken in them. We then realize that, in the unseen dimensions, we are connected to all living beings; and that the suffering we inflict on others is inflicted also to ourselves. Conversely, all the love, light and happiness we pour into their hearts become a spring of infinite joy in us.

For the consciousness to expand, purity is important, so that we become free of heavy thoughts and feelings. When we decide to live a pure life, which means giving the body the best living plant-based food, holding the best feelings in our hearts for ourselves and for others, and projecting by thought the best intentions towards all creatures, we then create the most favorable conditions for our advancement and blossoming. Of course, this requires constant work, because keeping watch against disturbing elements is quite a science. We must be conscious of the choices we make, for they influence our entire lives. What we watch (movies, TV programs); what we listen to (music, lectures), what we read, and even objects around us, the ambiance and people we visit—everything has an impact and influences us consciously or unconsciously.

That is why it is preferable to surround ourselves with harmonious objects, to choose the best music that elevates us, to befriend people who have a higher ideal than just working for themselves, to purify our actions and words, to send the best thoughts and feelings to all beings. This clears and beautifies the world so we feel useful and bring goodness all around us.

By deciding to improve our behavior and way of living, not only do we develop and perfect ourselves, but we also become free from the limitations of the physical plane. The freer we are, the more we move away from these dormant states of consciousness to elevate ourselves to the divine light.

It is up to us to study, go beyond ourselves and work inwardly to reach higher degrees in our understanding of morality, of the laws of nature and of the role we have to play during our passage on Earth, be it on an individual, familial, social or planetary level.

If we do not have the possibility of surrounding ourselves with the purest and most luminous things, what can prevent us from doing so mentally? The powers of the imagination are unlimited. If at times we feel that it is impossible and impractical in the present conditions to work on ourselves, let us consider all the means Cosmic Intelligence puts at our disposal to transform the difficulties that we meet. Instead of complaining about these situations, we can use them consciously to perfect ourselves and to develop qualities and virtues such as patience, humility, detachment, generosity, intelligence, dedication, etc.

When faced with obstacles and worries in daily life, instead of running away or taking refuge in nostalgia and deception, we can react by saying "Here is a new opportunity to evolve, to transform these inconveniences into positive elements." We are not obliged to remain in suffering, feeling sorrow, inner turmoil and being discontent because we have the power to change everything, to elevate ourselves above earthly conditions. If we do this work regularly, gradually, peace will eventually prevail, and our lives will become more harmonious.

We have hundreds of occasions to add a spiritual element to what we do. For example, when we prepare a meal, we can add a magical ingredient: our love. We can also think that those who eat this food will feel satisfied and, beyond the physical elements, they will also receive particles of health, joy, harmony and enthusiasm that we imagined while preparing the meal.

When we wash objects, we can also wash all the negative thoughts and feelings we experience on that day. I know a wonderful person who works as a cleaner in a hospital. She told me that each time she cleans a room, she imagines cleaning (symbolically) all the suffering in that place so the next patient can benefit from an atmosphere favorable for healing. She said she does it for every room and feels a great satisfaction, and never feeling tired. Isn't that wonderful?

There are so many ways to use the power of our thoughts, to express our love and make a difference in the daily lives of those who are close to us. For example, when we visit a family member or friends, on the way there, we can send them thoughts of joy, happiness, beauty and harmony so they are happy and recharged, and that our presence brings them an uplifting energy.

When we go for a walk, contemplate nature or watch a spring flowing, we can imagine that this water also flows in us, cleaning all impurities that prevent us from being happy. We can also imagine that the water springs from within us as enthusiasm, generosity and selfless love.

Everywhere and anytime of the day, we can do a divine work: during our commute to work, while waiting for an appointment, during our repose, when listening to music, rocking our children and even kissing our beloved. We can add a spiritual element through our thoughts, elevating us above the physical plane and linking us to the higher planes while influencing positively those around us at the same time.

However, there is a time that is the most favorable to do this work, that surpasses all others and that is at sunrise. In the peace, calm and silence of dawn, we find the best conditions to concentrate, meditate, contemplate and work on ourselves. During this unique, majestic and wonderful spectacle, our solar plexuses open, our hearts fill with joy, and our consciousnesses can expand to infinity because the light is the most sublime food for our soul and spirit.

Becoming a solar model

The sun is an unlimited source of energy and presently, thanks to the solar thermal and photovoltaic power plants throughout the world, its energy is stored and transformed into heat, cold and electricity. If we understood the importance of the sunrays as a renewable energy, why not use them as a resource, a model in our spiritual practice?

In the teaching of the philosopher and Master Omraam Mikhaël Aïvanhov, the sun and the heliocentric viewpoint are at the core of his philosophy. The sun, symbolically speaking, is the most perfect image of the Divinity. It is the heart of our universe, the inexhaustible source of life that lights, warms, purifies and vivifies all beings. It gives its light, warmth and life to all beings on Earth without judgement or discrimination. "It is the most powerful model that shows us the way to what is the purest, the most luminous and sublime." (Lecture of July 12, 1965)

The sun represents the spiritual aspect in us, the most divine part of our being, our higher Self composed of love, wisdom, power and virtues. Through meditation, prayer and contemplation, through exercises involving the imagination and identification, we can reconnect with that part of ourselves. Omraam Mikhaël Aïvanhov states that "by going to the sunrise every morning, we come closer to the center of life, God himself, and we move toward our own center so that our intelligence becomes more luminous, our heart discovers joy and peace, and our spirit becomes strong and free." (Lectures of October 18 and 30, 1960)

When the sun rises, all life awakens. In nature birds sing, and human beings begin their activities. Nothing is comparable to a sunrise and even though this spectacle has taken place hundreds of times before my eyes, it always feels like I see it for the first time. When I think again about all those blessed moments when, during a spiritual congress at the domain of Bonfin[73], we climbed in silence to the Rock of Prayer at dawn, I relive those unique and incomparable moments.

At times, it was still dark, and lifting our eyes to the sky, we could contemplate the last stars shining before the sky transformed into orange hues. The air was pure and cool. Dressed warmly and wrapped in our blankets, we settled into the lotus position to better concentrate. It was a magic moment blessed by the presence of our Master. In this peaceful and silent state, we breathed deeply and stayed fully attentive to receive the first rays of the sun. As the sun approached the horizon, an increased glow filled the sky and, like a pure shining diamond, the first rays caressed our faces in a moment of grace.

Rising above the world, the majestic and royal sun was flooding us with its powerful light. The life particles that floated in the morning air were penetrating us, and with each breath, a subtle energy filled us with

---

[73] Bonfin is located on the French Riviera and is the international congress center of the Universal White Brotherhood.

strength, joy and warmth. Our whole being felt this light, plus a profound and sincere gratitude toward this Cosmic Intelligence that created such beauty, poetry and wealth for all life.

No other experience is comparable to this grandiose spectacle; it is truly a communion with the divine world, with the spirit of Christ who, according to initiatic science, lives in the sun. This experience of bathing consciously in the waves produced by the sun must be lived at least once in a lifetime, absorbing its light, vibrating with it, looking at it with love and drinking (symbolically) its rays imagining that the light penetrates and purifies our being. It is a new method among the best to obtain extraordinary inner transformations! In the book *The Splendour of Tiphareth*, Omraam Mikhaël Aïvanhov gives several exercises to practice at sunrise.

By concentrating on the light, we can let it enter our minds and imagine it radiating to all the cells of the brain, driving away any negative thoughts. After, we can bring it to the heart, imagining it cleansing all the negative emotions such as sorrow, suffering, possessiveness, jealousy, sadness and deception, and replacing them with feelings of joy, happiness and peace. We can also bring it to the lungs and draw unlimited energies to renew our forces and become livelier and more resistant.

We can also send this light not only to the people we love—our family, children, friends, colleagues—but also to our employers, to the politicians, to all those who suffer and to those who seek and hope. In doing this work we feel that our hearts are bursting with joy, that the light is increasing in us, that our consciousness is expanding to infinity, and that the love we project is limitless and reaches out to the entire world.

Each morning at sunrise, we have the best conditions to do this exercise, to link with all the beings that surpass us, asking them to come and inspire us, and even to come and dwell in us, assisting us to be transformed and to become models of love, wisdom, goodness, integrity and honesty.

By doing this exercise each day, we notice deep changes and feel wonderful results. Imagine how your day can be after living such moments of grace. All day long, you feel the clarity, light, warmth and love. The transformations that this practice brings are so indescribable because when we contemplate the sun, we become a little like it: alive, expressive, warm and luminous. We feel uplifted, inspired, and rich, and we are prompted to distribute all this richness to the whole world.

Yes, the sunbeams are like subtle gold, the life emanating is never the same, it is constantly renewed. When concentrating on this center, we can renew all our cells and find our own center, which means the spiritual sun within us. And like the sun, we become transmitters of the divine light by awakening our own Divinity and that in others, by enlightening them through knowledge, through the warmth of our love and vivifying them by our energy. We then become living prisms, solar models, and we accomplish goodness through our thoughts, words, gestures and actions. All our lives are improved, as well as the lives of those surrounding us.

It is by working with the light individually and collectively that all humanity can be transformed and that will be extraordinary. If we participate in this grandiose work, if by our attitude and our radiance we contribute to helping and supporting those dear to us, and beyond that, all those who are linked to us in the invisible world, we can hope that one day harmony and peace will be established on the whole planet.

Loving to become free

We all know about the love that brings joy and temporary satisfaction at the beginning, but which, after a while, turns into quarrels, deception, suffering and sadness. Sometimes this love leaves profound wounds from which much time is needed to recover. We may lose our enthusiasm, confidence and candor, even feeling destroyed with a painful sense of betrayal and a feeling that we lost everything. Disappointed, we close our hearts or look for someone else to console us with the hope that the next relationship will be better.

Often, stories repeat themselves and from one disappointment to the next, we end up feeling that this way of loving does not meet our expectations, does not make us happier and leaves us feeling empty. How can we believe that a limited love that wants to take and possess, that is jealous, egotistical and sensual, that keeps changing according to circumstances, can ever fill the heart and human soul? It is impossible.

So, how can we blossom and find happiness? Through the high ideal of developing a more spiritual love, a more selfless, altruistic, kind, unchangeable love that remains stable in all conditions and circumstances of life. By consciously trying to transform our thoughts, feelings, actions and our egotistical desires, and by tirelessly working at perfecting ourselves in all domains so we become useful to others, to consider them as we would like to be considered.

Spiritual love is impersonal, generous, fraternal and beneficial. It is based on purity, abnegation and sacrifice. When we open up to this divine, unlimited love, we rise, we become freer, we acquire extraordinary qualities and virtues of goodness, gentleness, self-mastery, humility, nobility, strength and harmony. In thinking of helping others, of comforting them, healing them, supporting them, and giving them tools and methods so they become freer, we participate in making life on Earth more beautiful.

Distancing ourselves from the possessive love that takes, ties and limits, and by transforming our present lives to become the creators of magnificent, noble and luminous things, we become the conductors of divine love for others. When those we love blossom, become more beautiful, luminous, purer, more serene, more joyous and freer, we can then conclude that the love we pour into their hearts and souls is spiritual and divine.

Master Omraam Mikhaël Aïvanhov tells us that love has thirty-five million degrees, and that we are bathed in this ocean of love night and day, but that we are not conscious of it. Love is a cosmic energy, distributed abundantly around us, everywhere in the air, light, water, food, etc. but we do not open our hearts and souls to it so it can transform our entire life. We remain closed when so many riches are available throughout the universe. Let us open our hearts, souls and spirits, let us light up the fire of divine love so this love can make everything beautiful. It brings life, joy, happiness, it heals the heart of its wounds, it strengthens, elevates us above the earthly limitations; and, more importantly it frees us because we become masters of ourselves, free from all dependencies, jealousy and covetousness. When this love penetrates us, all our lives are enhanced. We are not waiting to be loved; we decide to love whatever the circumstances.

This flow of love running through us brings blessings, joy, a spiritually rich life and beneficial energies. We become creators and the wealth that Cosmic Intelligence deposits in us can be expressed and reach all those who surround us. We then become an immutable source of joy, inspiration and happiness for the beings we meet.

Of course, it may seem difficult to renounce the satisfaction of certain pleasures and to replace them with more spiritual activities, but by practicing every day, we advance slowly but surely toward new states of consciousness, new sensations of peace, of joy, happiness and liberty. Nothing holds us back from the limits of the ego because this constant flow of love sweeps away and rejects all impurities, negative states, sadness and sorrows. Indeed, all is washed, cleansed and purified within us, making room for harmony, peace, serenity, gentleness and calmness.

Master Omraam Mikhaël Aïvanhov was telling us that true love is a state of consciousness, which means that he recommended we do everything with love: to think with love, to feel with love, to speak with love, to look with love, to eat with love, to work with love, to breathe with love and, particularly in the morning, to absorb with love the waves, light and warmth of the sun which, according to initiatic science, is the best representation of divine love on Earth.

Nothing is comparable to the love that the sun sends to the earth in the way of light, colors, energy, warmth and life. We can nourish ourselves with it, drink at its source, and feel totally fulfilled without the need of going down lower into more prosaic manifestations. In this mystic, cosmic, divine love, we can feel physically, psychically and spiritually renewed. We have the impression of living in a state of grace, to rediscover the true meaning of life and to love everybody.

This love can expand to infinity, travel through space without limitations and, thanks to this love, we can be in relation with all the luminous entities of the universe. We then come closer to a world of purity, harmony, peace, plenitude and extraordinary vibrations. In this great inner silence, we can merge with the universal soul, vibrate in harmony with it, find happiness, experience immensity and come closer to true beauty. It is a real resurrection, a magnificent state of grace, a feeling of constant wonder in which we desire nothing more than to give, help, and serve others in a feeling of absolute gratitude.

Yes, when we collectively experience love as a state of consciousness, we not only improve our lives, but also the lives of all the beings we are connected to. When we manifest this pure and noble love, thinking of the wellbeing of others more than our own, we elevate our vibrations and come closer to the inner Divinity. Then, we experience a profound peace, new centers open within us and we attain bliss, ecstasy. Our lives become consecrated, abandoned totally in a feeling of gratitude towards God and all creation.

Human beings will be the Third Testament

"I first told you that in the Old Testament, Moses presented the Lord as a boss, a director, as something terrible, vindictive, scary and that we are simply poor fellows who must obey, and so forth. Well, it was like that in the past then Jesus came and presented the Lord as a Father and that we were his children. That was a lot better. But still, He was so far and not within us yet. And now comes an epoch where, in the Third Testament, the Lord is presented as living within us as being love, light, strength, life. Ah! It will be a real revelation, a true formula and a veritable realization."[74]

In the future, all beings will be prepared to receive the new currents coming into the world, renewing the link with the divine world in order to manifest on Earth this world of harmony, peace and light we all aspire to without always being aware of it.

When we accept the philosophy, the order, the balance and the pure life of the Initiates, abandoning our old habits and using everything at our disposal to perfect ourselves, we will discover within ourselves a new being who will manifest as love in our hearts, wisdom in our intelligence and intense life in our willpower. It is by working on our own development that we give this being the possibility to be free from the dominance of the ego and that we discover a new consciousness, a new inner birth.

Then, we shall recognize that we bear within us the same nature as Christ, Jesus, Buddha and the great Masters of humanity. When we develop our souls and spirits, we come closer to this celestial nature, we become one with our inner Divinity and we can accomplish what the words of Jesus meant: "You are Gods" (Psalm 82, 6).

---

[74] Omraam Mikhaël Aïvanhov, lecture of August 29, 1981.

How will the new beings manifest?

These new beings, linked to a higher consciousness, will manifest love, goodness, justice, compassion and tolerance. They will act with wisdom, gentleness and humility. They will vivify everything within and around them. They will radiate and live with enthusiasm, and wherever they go they will leave positive energies and imprints of light, joy and hope. They will be different because their ideal is beneficial for them and for the entire collectivity. Their actions will count more than their words, for in the new life, it is not so much about acquiring intellectual knowledge but living and manifesting their philosophy on Earth.

The new beings will have the knowledge of the universal laws and the laws of nature. They will understand and apply these rules. They will focus their efforts on improving their way of life not only for themselves but also to have a beneficial influence on all those around them and all those who are part of this vast living organism of humanity. Since we represent the cells of this universal organism, we must work not just for ourselves but for ALL, for everyone, for all nations and all beings who are part of the great cosmic body.

By incarnating on Earth, we accepted to learn, to grow and improve. Earth is a school where we come to learn to surpass ourselves and to evolve. The lessons of life are at times difficult and it often happens that we have to repeat the same experiences several times to understand our mistakes, our weaknesses and even our failures. But we have the responsibility to get up, stand, improve and expand our awareness so we don't vegetate and fall into inertia. It is up to us to learn from these lessons, change our old viewpoints and accept the new currents to become new beings. We can no longer live in ignorance by refusing to admit that we are solely responsible for our destinies and, if we refuse to move forward, it is 'life' itself that will send us the necessary trials for our development. Initiations are now in our daily lives, and how we face them will determine our growth.

We always have the choice to fall apart and feel sorry for ourselves or to seize the occasion to reflect on what needs to improve in our lives. The more we face reality by trying to understand the meaning of these challenges, by acting rather than reacting, the more we become free to live in higher states of being. We then feel our emotions being purified, our intellect clearing, our willpower strengthening and our consciousness expanding. A vast world opens within us, grander and more celestial, a world where even little things find their importance and reason for being.

True initiation is an expansion of consciousness, an elevation, an illumination, a new understanding of the true meaning of life. And once we have understood certain laws, certain truths, we cannot revert back. We can only go forward, relinquishing our ordinary lives, our weaknesses, moving upward to keep the flame of divine love alight and finding the inner synarchy.[75]

One day, everyone will understand the advantage of living a pure life filled with love and wisdom, the importance of cultivating inner harmony so it can manifest on Earth. It is this harmony that will bring the conditions to establish a new world. We can all participate in this glorious purpose.

By respecting and considering the forces of nature, by studying the great universal laws and by understanding the principles that govern our lives, we can penetrate the great mysteries of the world around us. It is by observing these laws that we can make a change in the whole world.

By sending positive mental vibrations to all creatures in a fraternal spirit, not only will we feel the benefits for ourselves, but we will also contribute to purifying the mental plane and the psychic atmosphere of the entire planet.

By developing our love toward all beings and by manifesting joy, enthusiasm, altruism, compassion, goodness, spirit of sacrifice and devotion, our hearts will not only be filled with joy, but we will have a positive influence on our friends, our family, our environment and all those around us.

By developing our willpower to manifest on a daily basis the virtues and qualities we would like to see in others, and by working on ourselves so that all our cells vibrate in harmony with the divine will, we will become a radiating and inspiring focal point for all beings.

Humanity needs to have awakened people who have developed a collective consciousness, who have become living models of this new world

---

[75] In the Teaching of Master Omraam Mikhaël Aïvanhov, the word 'synarchy' refers to the mastery of oneself: one's thoughts, feelings and actions.

where the spirit of universal fraternity reigns, beings who are fulfilled, who are beneficial and useful for the entire world.

The most sublime ideal is to rediscover this state of consciousness where our inner Divinity is paramount. Through meditation, prayer, contemplation and identification, we can develop other faculties and spiritual centers, liberating ourselves of egocentric desires and discovering, once again, the divine splendor and perfection Cosmic Intelligence deposited within us all.

"In the third Testament, it will be 'Do not ask and you shall receive, do not seek and you shall find, do not knock and it shall be open unto you.' When will this happen? When we become a fully developed child of God. Then, we shall no longer need to ask, to seek or to knock. We will live in plenitude."[76]

The new culture and the spirit of fraternity

At present, humanity is at an impasse on the economic, social, environmental and political fronts. The urgency to protect nature, to limit the waste of essential resources is obvious; otherwise, humanity is heading toward an imminent catastrophe. We all have the moral responsibility to act consciously because the earth is our common space. If we wish for an equitable sharing of the common resources, we must become aware that all our gestures, thoughts, feelings and emotions are reflected on our environment. It is time to reflect and to realize that our excesses, our overconsumption on all levels produce pollution, some physical and psychic waste affecting the needs of others and generating social iniquities and injustices.

Recently, the coronavirus pandemic demonstrated how fragile the world balance is and that it can collapse in a very short time. We are living a historical moment in the life of humanity, and this world crisis proves that great changes are needed. We become aware that the time of separateness is over. It is time to unite for the wellbeing of all; to cultivate altruism, a spirit of fraternity and international solidarity. May our goodwill, intelligence, knowledge and abilities be at the service of others for the wellbeing of the collectivity. The interdependence that connects us all is evident not only

---

[76] Omraam Mikhaël Aïvanhov, lecture of April 8, 1977.

on the physical plane but on all levels. It is time to develop a new collective consciousness, a culture of help, support, natural cooperation and universal fraternity, so that all members of the human family are united.

A new cycle is presently beginning. New possibilities and methods are available to transform ourselves and the entire planet. It is only up to us to grasp the opportunity and open ourselves to this world of harmony and balance, becoming aware that we have the power to change things, for both our happiness and that of future generations. We are on the threshold of a new era where each and every one has an important role to play. Our values and vision are changing; we are beginning to understand that everything in our universe is linked and connected in a perfect unity. We are all interdependent, and together we can succeed in building a harmonious destiny for all humanity.

This future shall be splendid, marvelous and sublime but, it is now that we ought to build it. If we use all the amazing faculties Cosmic Intelligence deposited in everyone to participate in the emergence of this extraordinary Golden Age, sooner or later, it will come. And we can do so by first imagining and creating it through our thoughts, wishing it with all our hearts, and finally by changing our way of living. At first, we will feel the changes within us, but then subsequently, it will spread to the whole planet.

Everything is possible if we have the knowledge, faith, love and goodwill.

This ideal of universal peace between all beings, of liberty, respect of nature, of cooperation between nations can be achieved if all of us, collectively, become aware that our true interest is not in the material world but way higher up in the values of the spiritual world. If we understand that true spirituality is not about escaping or leaving the earth but, quite the contrary, to transform this planet into a wonderful place where all beings can live in brotherhood and sisterhood. By linking with our inner higher being, we walk toward this Christic love and find the splendor, beauty and divine perfection that Cosmic Intelligence put in and around each one of us. One day, everything that is luminous will become reality. We will have extraordinary exchanges which will be more subtle and more intense with all beings. We will stand in wonder and marvel at the wealth contained within each person.

At that moment, all beings will reach inner higher summits, individually and collectively experiencing joy, happiness and celestial plenitude. One day, the spirit of fraternity will appear to Earth and we shall live in a Christic state of consciousness, a state of divine love, wisdom and inspiration.

How long will it take to realize this on Earth? It doesn't matter…

For the great Initiates, this state of consciousness is already realized, for others, it will come, and for some, it remains utopic and distant.

How about you? Do you believe in it? Personally, I do!

Biography:

Henriette Dufeu has a background in piano and classical guitar, which she has taught for many years. Interested from her youth in meditation and the study of the esoteric science, in 1978, at the age of 21, she discovered the Teaching of Master Omraam Mikhaël Aïvanhov, who presents the greatest spiritual truths in a simple, clear and accessible way. She then deeply felt the need to go to France to meet this Master.

From 1978 to 1986, she lived at his spiritual school which became the most important moment of her existence. She discovered the real meaning of life, the true initiatic science that explains the structure of a human being, the methods and exercises to transform oneself, as well as the work on the light and the correspondences between the visible and invisible, the subtle and tangible worlds.

After 8 years of studying at that mystical school, she returned to Quebec.

In 1988, she became the managing director and co-owner of the bakery Dufeu along with her husband, in Sherbrooke, Quebec.

"I was 21 years old when Master Omraam Mikhaël Aïvanhov gave me this advice: 'Never stop loving, always expand your love; love all beings, nature, the whole world, angels, archangels and the entire universe. Love as Initiates do, without expecting anything in return, and always choose the best, choose the best conditions for your soul.'"

CHAPTER 8

PROPHECIES AND BEATITUDES

by
Carmen Froment

In this chapter we will explore the different prophecies made in the last century, which link the present period to the coming one, and into the far future. These prophecies are from great thinkers, Initiates and Masters. It is not a matter of defining who is right or which position they hold in the hierarchy. All true Initiates and Masters work together to realize their mission and that is to participate in the realization of the Kingdom of God on Earth. In modern times this has come to be known as the realization of the Golden Age, in which everyone will recognize themselves as children of the same Celestial Father and the same Divine Mother regardless of race, color, language or country.

In recent years the last prophecies of Master Peter Deunov (Beinsa Douno) have been circulating on the Internet in English and in French. But, according to an article published by doctors Robert Powell and Harrie Salman,[77] these prophecies are not always an accurate translation from Bulgarian and are not all of the last words of the Master. They are rather a compilation taken from some of his last words during 1944 and also from earlier texts. Let us remember that Master Peter Deunov was born in July 1864 and departed in December 1944.

---

[77] https://sophiafoundation.org/wp-content/uploads/2020/06/Prophecy-of-Peter-Deunov-Beinsa-Douno.pdf

In his research Dr. Robert Powell states that, according to Peter Deunov, the age of Kali Yuga (a period of approximately 5000 years) began in 4471 BCE and lasted until 1999[78]. It represented the involution period of humanity. Whereas Rudolf Steiner indicates that the period of Kali Yuga ranged from 3101 BCE to 1899, when the earth entered the Satya Yuga, the age of enlightenment, the evolution period of humanity. It is appropriate to mention here that Rudolf Steiner, considered a great Initiate, was born in 1861 and departed for the other world in 1925 and was therefore a contemporary of Master Peter Deunov.

Kali Yuga is known as the iron age, a dark age in which material life rules and the spiritual life is nearly absent. Kali Yuga is part of the great cosmic cycle humanity agreed to undergo in order to ultimately triumph over matter and reintegrate the lost paradise of our souls and spirits. It is known as a difficult time, a descent into matter, a period of egoism and suffering.

However, according to the Hindu calendar (which corresponds to the contemporary analysis of the historical data given by Bibhu Dev Misra[79]) and taking into account the precession of the earth's axis[80] calculated at 30% by the most versed in the field, a transition of 300 years indicates that Kali Yuga would have ended possibly around 200 years ago or will end in the next 100 years. When taking into consideration the human condition at present, it is easy to think that we are still deep in this dark age.

One way or another, we are in the core of a profound transformation for humanity. No doubt that we are at a crossroads: the choice is to persist in this dark age and risk the annihilation of the planet and humanity, or move toward an age of awakening, of inner light, and make the planet a garden of paradise. The return of Christ—the Christ spirit—takes place on an etheric level and in our consciousness according to Steiner. And at each great turning point, be it on an individual or planetary level, we undergo a series of trials or initiations that test the progress of our evolution. The

---

[78] Peter Deunov – Prorokut, Stara Zagora 2009, p. 239.
[79] https://grahamhancock.com/dmisrab6
[80] In astronomy, axial precession is a gravity-induced, slow, and continuous change in the orientation of an astronomical body's rotational axis. In particular, it refers to the gradual shift in the orientation of Earth's axis of rotation in a cycle of approximately 25,772 years. Wikipedia.

same applies to cultures. As we read in the chapter covering RACES and Cultures, the earth has undergone several metamorphoses. Like a caterpillar which turns into a chrysalis and emerges as a butterfly, it is our turn to come out of the materialistic cocoon and learn to unfurl our wings and fly toward the light. In the past, different elements in nature participated in this human metamorphosis, such as water at the time of the great floods, and now it is the fire element which will play the greatest role. We can already observe this by the fires that burn ever more frequently and severely on the planet.

It is interesting to see how the fire element correlates with the new, rising culture which will be one of love. A universal, celestial love and more especially, because it is fire, the sacred fire of divine love that has the task of purifying the human heart. If we befriend this fire, if we invite it to set our hearts ablaze, to find an abode in our souls, we are protected and have nothing to fear. This observation and the undeniable truth of it have arisen through a personal experience of mine that occurred two years ago. A terrible thunderstorm had broken out in the area where we live, and forest fires ignited where lightning had struck. Over the next few days great winds continued to spread the fires, bringing them ever closer to our area, and we were put on an evacuation alert. Already the smoke was so dense that we took refuge in our homes in order to breathe better. Neighbors were already moving their horses, alpacas, donkeys and other animals to farms further away. Friends were calling and inviting us to leave our home to go and stay with them. It was late at night and the essentials were ready by the door in case the evacuation was ordered. I decided to meditate before trying to fall asleep and the following came to mind: "Angel of fire, you know how I appreciate you, how I contemplate you each morning at sunrise and beg you to light your sacred fire in me. I am your ally. I am your friend. In essence, I am of the same nature as you and so, I beg you to protect us." To my great surprise, we learned the next morning that the wind had completely changed direction during the night, that the fire had folded into itself and was slowly dying out. I was astonished and filled with a profound sense of gratitude. So I keep in my heart the conviction that the fire element has its work to perform, that it acts on the directives of much higher Beings who in turn watch over the planet and human beings. It is by linking with these Beings and by nurturing the desire to improve, to evolve and to perfect ourselves that we attract their protection and their blessings.

Let us now come back to this sacred fire and see what Master Peter Deunov had to say about it:

> All earthly beings will be subject to the great purification of the 'divine fire' to become worthy of the new epoch. Even if all human beings are not at the same point in their development, this renovator 'fire' will leave no one unscathed. This wave of life is powerful as a means of transformation which simultaneously takes place on planet Earth and in the cosmos.
>
> A powerful magnetic current coming from cosmic space, with the power of millions of volts, has already reached the Earth, spreading at great speed over the whole world.
>
> Those who are not prepared to face this current will have great nervous shocks, physical discomfort and different psychic ailments.
>
> These waves from cosmic space will manifest periodically. According to peoples' inner state, positive or negative, they will affect their blood by weakening it or thickening it, they will strengthen or weaken their nervous system.
>
> The only thing to do at present is to learn to be in harmony with the waves of the new life coming to Earth. All individuals who are aware and reasonable must elevate the vibrations of their thoughts and make their feelings nobler through a constant union with God. They must feel the reality of the Eternal Source of all life; they must rejoice, be ever thankful, and pray.[81]

---

[81] Beïnça Douno, *L'Enseignement de vie Nouvelle*, Le Courrier du Livre, éd. 1983 p. 238 (our translation).

Among the last words of Master Peter Deunov were these predictions for humanity:

> The Earth now enters the new, divine conditions. The whole world is awakening. The one who desires to remain in the old conditions can do so. The whole world, the whole solar system and whole universe, everything is moving in a new direction. Human consciousness is expanding. You will be witnesses to that Great Expansion; you will be witnesses to that Great Transformation for which God now prepares the whole of humankind. The world will come to know that God shall not be mocked.[82]

> For thousands of years the Earth has been passing through a zone of space which is full of poison. The entire solar system has been passing through that region. There was another system in that place which passed away long ago but its dust has remained, and it poisons all beings in the solar system with the exception of a few of those on the Sun itself. [...] This is a sphere of great contradictions. Now we are approaching the end of the sphere—soon we shall exit this sphere of the Universe (the 13th sphere). So much blood, so many tears![83]

> Our solar system will depart from heavier matter and enter into a less dense medium. Because of this, there will exist conditions for the manifestation of a higher consciousness for humankind. The solar system departs from the so-called '13th sphere'. At the same time, the Sun will enter the Age of Aquarius. Now is the end of the dark epoch, the Kali Yuga.[84]

---

[82] Beinsa Douno *The Wellspring of Good – The Last Words of Master Beinsa Douno*, Sofia, 2013, p. 212.

[83] Beinsa Douno, *Sacred words of the Master*, 2004, pp. 215-216.

[84] Beinsa Douno *The Wellspring of Good – The Last Words of Master Beinsa Douno*, Sofia, 2013, p. 292.

Modern times cannot be compared to the future that is coming. Now a nucleus of people from all nations is forming in the world. English, French, German, Russian, American, Japanese, Chinese, Bulgarian, Turk, Serb, and so on, are forming a new race, a nation with a new understanding, which is different from the present. Who unites these spirits? The Great Divine Law attracts them that they may come to know one another and work together.[85]

Each race is characterized by certain qualities. Black people are notable for their imagination and strong feelings; the native peoples of the Americas [red race] for their ability to apply geometry and mathematics. Asians [yellow race] are notable for their objective mind and Caucasians [white race] for their rationality: ever since they have been on Earth, they have been measuring and exploring things with precision. The sixth race expected to develop in the future has all the good qualities of the preceding races. In this regard, it represents the essential synthesis of the human virtues.[86]

In our research about the 6th RACE, it is said that it will be the race of Love: a generous, impersonal and sublimated Love. At last it will be the Kingdom of God on Earth, where humanity will live harmoniously as brothers and sisters and all will recognize each other as souls and not merely as bodies. It shall be the fraternity of souls. The faculty of thought will be used for its creative and constructive role. Human beings will reincarnate of their own free will and not simply based on their karma. In all aspects, choices will be greater since everything will be at the service of the soul.

Those whose consciousness is awakened have already begun to inwardly experience the Golden Age or the Kingdom of God. In consciousness they

---

[85] Id. pp. 370-372.
[86] Emilie Michael, *Sealed by the Sun, Life between Rudolf Steiner and Peter Deunov*, p. 315.

are ahead of the present culture and form the stem of the 6ᵗʰ RACE. It is not necessary to wait for thousands of years to taste what is coming or to live the new life. The higher Beings who watch over humanity are only waiting for us and for our call in order to come and help us, to support us and elevate us to their vision of reality.

In the writings of Edgar Cayce

The brilliant American clairvoyant Edgar Cayce (1877-1945) became clairvoyant at the early age of ten when he would fall asleep while trying to learn his lessons. A few minutes after waking up, he could recite entire pages, as if read through photographic memory. These states of mediumship (readings) became his mission. He answered thousands of questions about health, professions, reincarnations, human history, Earth's geographic changes and so on.

According to his research, Cayce confirmed what Masters Peter Deunov, Omraam Mikhaël Aïvanhov and Rudolf Steiner have all said: that Russia would play an important role in the future.

Between the years 1921 and 1944, Edgar Cayce gave twenty-nine readings which have been grouped into the series #3976 under the name: *Readings on world affairs*. On two occasions, in 1932 and 1944, he predicted that Russia would indeed play an important role in the future of humanity.

The two readings correlate the same information, but the one of June 22, 1932 (#3976-29) goes into more detail, confirming our research:

> What then of nations? In Russia there comes the hope of the world, not as that sometimes termed of the Communistic, of the Bolshevistic; no. But freedom, freedom! That each man will live for his fellow man! The principle has been born. It will take years for it to be crystallised, but out of Russia comes again the hope of the world.

The readings given by this remarkable medium rarely predict future events, because he usually answered specific questions and he did not offer more than what was asked. He said that the future is in continual movement. He affirmed that his predictions were based on the conditions of the moment, but that people could change the future by their willpower. It is important to remember that collectively we create what we each entertain in our thoughts, feelings and actions. Edgar Cayce also attested that peace begins within.

One day, in a lecture by Master Omraam Mikhaël Aïvanhov, we heard the following:

> Toward the end of his life Peter Deunov had gathered several people and told them: 'Jesus brought the principles, myself the methods, and Mikhaël will realize.' Many people wrote this to me, and I still have the letters in Bulgarian.[...] But realize what? Oh, a little room here with a few people! No, no, he did not say this: he will realize the Golden Age. Well, one had to understand! Therefore, his words come close to what the Puranas say. And this I kept for myself for 45 years, even more, 55 years! And I reveal it to you now. Again, I repeat exactly the same, and if I mislead you, what a punishment! And myself, I do not want to be punished! I tell you the truth. 'And Mikhaël will realize'. Neither Moses, nor Buddha, Krishna, Hermes Trismegistus or Orpheus; none of these great, great spirits realized the Golden Age. [87]

In another lecture from July 22, 1980, Master Omraam pronounced the following:

> Steiner said: 'I bring you a Teaching and my language is a bit difficult. But someone will come after me, who will speak clearly, under the sign of enthusiasm, and he will bring the Mikhaëlic era.' There will be a new epoch, Steiner was not mistaken.

---

[87] Excerpt from a lecture of Omraam Mikhaël Aïvanhov dated April 25, 1982 (our translation).

In August 1921, Rudolf Steiner indicated that a Bodhisattva was born at the beginning of the century or around 1900, whose activity would manifest around 1936 and who would become the future Maitreya Buddha.[88] Who was the great being born in 1900, and began his public activity around 1936?

When human beings awaken, they take charge of their evolution and assume the responsibility for such, knowing where their true interests lie. They do not hesitate to dedicate time to the expansion of their souls and the vivifying of their spirits.

To conclude this chapter and the present book on an inspiring note, we would like to share with you the beatitudes as expressed by Master Omraam Mikhaël Aïvanhov[89]:

> May the Angels and Archangels now open the floodgates and pour out their generosity on the children of God, on all humankind. May there be an abundance of light and understanding, an abundance of joy and happiness so that humankind may, at last, accomplish the exalted mission for which it is on Earth: to reflect and express the Creator and the beauty of Heaven.
>
> Blessed are those who are aware of this
>
> Blessed are those who are consumed by this sacred fire
>
> Blessed are those who have made up their minds to be conductors of their heavenly Father
>
> Blessed are those who are the meek
>
> Blessed are those who know peace
>
> Blessed are those who want to work and make sacrifices

---

[88] Consult p. 38 of the following website: https://sophiafoundation.org/wp-content/uploads/2020/06/Prophecy-of-Peter-Deunov-Beinsa-Douno.pdf

[89] Omraam Mikhaël Aïvanhov, Complete Works, *The Splendour of Tiphareth: The Yoga of the Sun*, pp.118-119, Prosveta S.A.

Blessed, blessed, blessed be the children of the Universal White Brotherhood!

Bonfin, August 12, 1967

Biography: see Carmen's biography in the chapter entitled: The Medicine of the Future.

ABOUT THE AUTHORS

The Aquarian Team

Meet the authors of this 3rd book

Annie Collet, France

Olivier Picard, France

Carmen Froment, Canada
coordinator

Carla Machado, Brazil

Pascale Frémond, Canada

Dorette Chappuis, Switzerland

Henriette Dufeu, Canada

ACKNOWLEDGEMENTS

Thanks to an extraordinary teamwork, our 3rd book is seeing the light of day during a unique time when the entire globe is subject to conditions never experienced before in regards to this pandemic. While everyone was confined to their homes, we were afforded excellent conditions to work on our chapters and to collaborate via the Internet.

We owe an immense debt of gratitude to each person on the team for doing their part and at times going above and beyond what was required of them. It was truly a collective spirit that sustained us in the true spirit of Aquarius, the water bearer, who quenches thirst on all levels.

Thank you to our families, our husbands, partners, brothers and sisters (family and soul family), our friends and dear ones. We did not forget you despite the numerous hours spent in front of the computer screen.

Thank you to Balboa Press for welcoming another one of our books. We certainly hope that this 3rd book will be the yeast that will nourish the inner dough rising in the souls of our readers.

And our appreciation goes without saying to our instructor, who guided us while he was alive and who keeps guiding us from the spiritual spheres. The Aquarian Team

Note:

All authors and reviewers have donated their valuable time and skills for free. Moreover, the authors have agreed to donate all profits from the book sales to charitable organizations.

Invitation:

We invite you to visit our website for updates and news about the team: www.theaquarianteam.com, our YouTube channel for talks and to like our Facebook page: The Aquarian Team.

You may also request to be added to the subscribers list for our inspiring, free monthly e-newsletter at: newsletter@theaquarianteam.com

References:

Books and DVDs: www.prosveta.com (with references in many languages)

Universal White Brotherhood: http://www.fbu.org/site_anglais/general_english/name.htm

Lectures of Omraam Mikhaël Aïvanhov on YouTube: www.youtube.com/watch?v=BxCy2GjZKxw

Printed in the United States
by Baker & Taylor Publisher Services